THE PUEBLO POTTER

A STUDY OF CREATIVE IMAGINATION
IN PRIMITIVE ART

BY

RUTH L. BUNZEL

DOVER PUBLICATIONS, INC., NEW YORK

TO MY MOTHER

Published in Canada by General Publishing Company, Ltd., 30 Lesmill Road, Don Mills, Toronto, Ontario.

Published in the United Kingdom by Constable and Company, Ltd., 10 Orange Street, London WC 2.

This Dover edition, first published in 1972, is an unabridged republication of the work originally published by Columbia University Press, New York, in 1929.

International Standard Book Number: 0-486-22875-4
Library of Congress Catalog Card Number: 72-79159

Manufactured in the United States of America
Dover Publications, Inc.
180 Varick Street
New York, N. Y. 10014

CONTENTS

ACKNOWLEDGMENTS

The material upon which the following study is based was collected in the course of two seasons' work in the pueblos of New Mexico and Arizona during the summers of 1924 and 1925. It is part of an investigation of various aspects of pueblo life pursued under the auspices of the Southwest Society and the Department of Anthropology of Columbia University.

It is impossible to name within the brief compass of a preface all those who have contributed in one way or another to the making of this book. Above all the author feels her inability to find adequate expression of her indebtedness to her beloved teacher, Franz Boas, for his guidance and inspiration. His rigorous scholarship has set the standard and his zeal and encouragement have been the spur. Only less is her debt to her teacher and co-worker, Ruth Fulton Benedict. To Dr. Elsie Clews Parsons she is indebted for the opportunity to enlarge the scope of the study beyond its original plan, and for valuable practical advice on field technique.

Dr. Clark Wissler and the late Dr. Pliny E. Goddard of the American Museum of Natural History, Dr. Walter Hough of the United States National Museum, Dr. Berthold Laufer and Dr. Ralph Linton of the Field Museum, Dr. W. Willoughby of the Peabody Museum, Mr. Kenneth Chapman of the State Historical Museum of Santa Fe, Dr. Mira of Santa Fe and Dr. A. V. Kidder of Andover, have all been of inestimable assistance in giving the author access to public and private collections of pottery, and in supplying much valuable information concerning the material contained therein. For this service she wishes to thank them all. And also all those many friends in the far corners of New Mexico and Arizona whose help and hospitality have made the way easy and pleasant.

Finally her deepest gratitude goes to the real makers of this book, the Indian artists for whom the author is but the mouthpiece. To them she is indebted for the materials out of which this book is made, for patient and generous coöperation in its making, and for the splendid example which they have held before her of the patient pursuit of perfection. She has tried to interpret their aspirations to an alien world. She trusts that she has not misrepresented them in any way. But if she has, their works will speak for them in a universal language.

R. L. B.

Columbia University
    April, 1929

LIST OF PLATES

ABBREVIATIONS

AMNH   American Museum of Natural History, New York

USNM   United States National Museum, Washington

I

INTRODUCTION

The world contains no people so crude in culture that they lack a decorative art. Almost the earliest remains of our cave-dwelling ancestors in Europe are bone implements incised with marks in regular sequence which serve no utilitarian purpose, but present a surface more pleasing to the eye than a plain expanse of undecorated bone. This is the earliest known art. Like language and social organization, art, the embellishment of objects and activities beyond the requirements of their ostensible purposes, has accompanied man since the dawn of history. Its origin is veiled in mystery; it lies behind the earliest known records. Whatever it may be, to whatever biological or psychological need of the organism art is the response, it must be recognized as one of the most constant forms of human behavior.

Like all other forms of human behavior, art forms are not the direct response of the individual to the esthetic impulse. It might be assumed that a man painting a box to contain his personal belongings, and wishing to adorn it in some fashion pleasing to himself, would use this opportunity for individual expression. To some extent he does this; yet even the individual of marked originality operates within narrow limits, limits much narrower than those set by the exigencies of the technique. These limits are socially determined, just as are the methods of designating kindred. Language in order to fulfill its function as symbols of communication must be cast into accepted forms. The need for formalizing expression in art is more difficult to understand; even among primitive peoples art is recognized as primarily an individual func-

tion. Yet the tendency of artistic activity to become set in definite modes of expression characteristic of different social groups is so marked that when ethnologists were seeking a convenient term by which to designate the socially determined limits of acceptable behavior, they borrowed the word "pattern" from the terminology of decorative art.

Decorative style may be defined as the mode of plastic expression characteristic of any group at any given time. The limits of acceptable expression, though always clearly definable, are constantly shifting. They may be gradually stretched to include within the lists of the approved expressions that yesterday were outlandish. Or some rarely gifted individual may override the established boundaries, remapping completely the field of esthetic activity. This shifting of familiar and recognized landmarks is as characteristic of the artistic development of primitive peoples as of our own.

It is with these fluctuations and mutations and the conditions which bring them about that the following pages will deal. This is a study especially of the manner in which an individual operates within the limits of an established style, or finding that impossible, creates new values and wins for them social recognition. It is an attempt to enter fully into the mind of primitive artists; to see their technique and style, not as they appear objectively to students of museum collections, but as these appear to the artists themselves, who are seeking in this field of behavior a satisfactory and intelligible technique of individual expression. For this reason no attempt will be made to give a complete, analytical description of primitive artistic products or techniques. The opinions of primitive artists are used wherever possible; museum material has been used sparingly.

The material upon which this study is based was gathered during two summers spent at Zuni and other pueblos of the Southwest of the United States, where a highly developed decorative art in pottery still flourishes. Most of the material was obtained through direct questioning, supplemented by observation of pottery making, criticism and instruction. The writer learned to make pottery in two different villages, trying as far as possible to conform to native standards. Methods of instruction, criticism of her work, and especially emphasis in teaching, provide some of the most interesting and valuable material.

Naturally the difficulties in the handling of so subtle a problem of primitive psychology are very great. Artists, even in more sophisticated societies, are notoriously inarticulate. The great mass of written and printed words about art are those not of artists but of critics of art. That primitive artists should be more articulate is not to be expected. Furthermore, it has been necessary for the most part to work through interpreters, or with women whose knowledge of English is fragmentary. Younger women whose command of English was satisfactory were mostly too completely Americanized to practise native arts. There was additional difficulty involved in the general pueblo attitude of intense hostility to all white people. This made Acoma and Santa Domingo practically unavailable for investigation.

There are, therefore, lamentable gaps in the material. Many of the most important problems must still remain unanswered, or at best only fragmentarily and inconclusively treated. The evidence on such important points as the character of dreamed designs and the role of the visual image and other non-rational processes in artistic creation, is far from satisfactory. We get but a fleeting glimpse into the subtle mysteries of creative imagination.

The scope of the investigation has been limited to the handling of decorative problems in the manufacture of household articles of clay. The solution of these problems is conditioned, as in other techniques, by the limitations of the material and the necessities of practicable form. However, the range of possibilities in ceramics is wider than in almost any other primitive technique. Compared, for instance, with basketry or work in stone, the limits imposed by the technique are slight.

Owing to the plastic nature of the material, almost any conceivable form is possible. Setting aside modelling in the round as outside the scope of the present investigation, and confining ourselves to practicable utensils, we find even in these an enormous range of possibilities. In aboriginal North America, pottery is made entirely by hand, so there is not even the limitation to circular forms which is inevitable where pottery is turned on the wheel. Square, box-like vessels can be made and are, in fact, still made in some places. An endless variety of curvilinear forms are possible. Furthermore, there are no definite limits to the size of vessels that can be made of clay. What limits there are, are set by the skill of the potter in mixing her materials, building the vessel and firing it, rather than by the inherent nature of the material. In the larger vessels the difficulty of firing increases out of all proportion to the size. Nevertheless, vessels of great size are still made by primitive potters. As the size of the vessel increases beyond a certain point, the range of forms becomes more restricted.

In addition to the esthetic values inherent in the basic forms of vessels, the plastic nature of the material may be utilized to produce decorative effects, in the stricter meaning of the term. Relief modelling, stamping, and incising are widely distributed decorative techniques of this category. The characteristic "corrugated" pottery of the Southwest is an unusual method of deriving ornament directly from the plasticity of the material.

Ceramic art offers a wide range of possibilities in the utilization of surface finish and color. Rough surfaces, smooth slips, polishes and glazes all have their esthetic values, and may be combined in ornamental effects. The use of glaze paint on smoothly slipped surfaces, and of dull paint on highly polished surfaces are known in this area.

Great variation is possible in the employment of color. White, gray, cream, buff, orange, red, and black have all been used as base colors at one time or another in the Southwest, and this by no means exhausts the possibilities afforded by the geological environment. No experiments have been made to determine the widest limits of the resources of the area; but even the most fragmentary collection of pottery representing different periods in the same place shows that the resources are not exploited even to the extent that they are known. Color in the form of painting, — the arrangement of contrasting colors in ornamental patterns — is the most common form of ornament in the Southwest. This may be, and frequently is, combined with other techniques of decoration, such as modelling and the ornamental use of glazes and polishes.

The foregoing is a brief outline of the possibilities of ceramic technique. What, now are its peculiar limitations? It is not our purpose to enter into a discussion of purely technical difficulties involved in the creation of a practical product. A first-rate piece of pottery, one that is light, strong, and watertight, is one of the great achievements in primitive technology. It represents the utilization of a large and complex body of technical knowledge concerning the properties of various clays, their most advantageous combination, the preparation of the paste, structural necessities in the building of vessels, and finally firing to just the requisite degree of hardness. There are numerous works on ceramics in which these matters are discussed. Dr. Guthe has described in detail the technology of pueblo pottery in his admirable book on the pottery of San Ildefonso.[1] It is not our purpose to discuss these problems, but to indicate rather the general limitations which ceramic technique places upon the creative imagination. It must

[1] Guthe, 1925.

be remembered always that the decorative style of any group is culturally determined. It is a selection which leaves a wide margin for variation within the limits of the technical potentialities. What is technically possible is not always esthetically possible.

In spite of what has been said above, ceramic products are, with rare exceptions, limited to circular forms. This is due to the greater ease in working and the greater strength of these shapes. Bowls and dishes are circular, rather than oval or square; jars tend to be globular, rather than cylindrical. Pottery is a fragile product at best, and gains in strength as corners are eliminated and the exposed surface in proportion to capacity is reduced. Furthermore, large vessels must be very carefully handled in the plastic state. They cannot be lifted, and so are set on a mold or board which can be turned while the surface is worked. Since pottery is essentially a household art, the forms of vessels are further limited by the purposes for which they are designed.

Of the decorative techniques only painting is definitely limited by geological environment. Modelling, incising, polishing are possible wherever clay is found. But the environment does not always offer clays in sufficient variety to make painting feasible.

There are, however, certain general esthetic limitations, that are far more important than those of a technical nature. Whatever technique of decoration is employed, the ornament must be applied to a continuous curved surface, and only pottery designs are successful which recognize both this curvature and continuity. This, in part, accounts for the wide distribution and persistence of banded designs on jars and bowl rims, and of radiating designs on bowl interiors. Horizontal seriation is by no means restricted to decorative art, much less to ceramic art. It is the common arrangement of natural phenomena. It is, however, especially appropriate in pottery because of the intimate relation of the horizontal band to the structure of the coiled clay vessel. Much modern pueblo pottery does not recognize this relation, and is therefore, esthetically inferior. There is something extremely offensive to sensitive critics in the essential disharmony between form and design in many modern Zuni pots.

The next great problem is that of fitting the pattern to the surface. Since the field is continuous, the pattern must be perfectly spaced to fill it without break. In painted and incised pottery errors in drawing can be corrected only with very great difficulty. The decoration of pottery requires therefore, not only a steady hand, and perfect coördination between hand and eye, but a very great sensitivity to spatial values. The difficulty of visualizing the design in relation to the surface is further increased by the fact that with but few exceptions the whole of the decorative field does not lie within the field of vision at one time. The importance of these problems in native consciousness, and the methods devised for their solution will become apparent in the following chapters.

Pottery has been made by the sedentary peoples of the American Southwest for at least two thousand years. Archaeologists have traced the history of the art from its crude beginnings through its period of greatest efflorescence and gradual decline. The contemporary product does not approach that of seven or eight centuries ago, in either technical or artistic excellence. Nevertheless, the art is by no means moribund. Pottery making is an important industry in a number of villages, each village producing a highly differentiated ware. The diversity is purely esthetic, for all current wares are based upon the same technique, and have grown up upon a common historical background. Ceramic history in the Southwest shows clearly the process of differentiation from the common ancestral type with increasing instability and local diversification in recent times. The causes which have led to the differentiation are not at present clearly understood. Certainly they were not simple. Development has been conditioned by both inner factors and outside influences. At present the whole region is passing through a period of great cultural instability, an instability which is naturally reflected in decorative art. The large amount of historical and comparative data which is available for study, against which the results of field investigation under changing conditions can be checked, makes this a particularly fruitful field in which to study processes of artistic development.

The esthetic values inherent in the material are no longer exploited to the extent to which they were in ancient times. Corrugated ware has disappeared completely; so has incised ornament, and modelled ornament has survived only in ceremonial pottery and can, therefore, be said to have disappeared as a decorative technique. Basic forms are also less varied than in former times. There has apparently been a decline in interest in form for its own sake. Each village makes a few standardized forms, their character largely determined by practical considerations. The one notable exception is the black ware of Santa Clara and San Ildefonso, where interest in form still lingers. These vessels still display a variety and subtlety of form that has all but disappeared in other places. Santa Clara potters also use ornament in the form of flutings and indentations, showing an appreciation of the decorative possibilities peculiar to work in clay.

Surface finish also receives less attention than in former times. Here again the one exception is at Santa Clara and San Ildefonso, where interest is concentrated upon the use of lustrous polish, both as body finish and as ornament. Elsewhere only smooth slipped and slightly polished surfaces are found. Ornament in glaze paint, once widely used, has been given up entirely.

The modern potter depends, therefore, almost entirely upon color for achieving her effects, and even here there has been considerable shrinkage. Red as a base color, although once common, is practically extinct. Each village clings to one body color, just as it makes only one type of water jar and one type of bowl. At Santa Clara and San Ildefonso, this is black, with red as a distinctly minor ware at San Idefonso; at Zuni,

Laguna and Acoma it is white; at Cochiti and Santo Domingo light buff; on First Mesa yellow, rarely red. The use of color as ornament is confined almost entirely to black, varying to brown, with small amounts of red, on a white or cream base. At Acoma, yellow is also used in a particular type of vessel; on First Mesa one can find a few pieces of black on red; at Zuni one woman has revived the ancient red ware, decorated with white and black. Painting shows none of the variety and subtlety in the handling of color found in the best prehistoric polychrome wares. The use of as many as eight colors on a single vessel was once common in the Zuni valley.

It is important to realize at the outset the very slight extent to which modern potters utilize known resources. It is neither lack of resources nor lack of knowledge that makes modern pueblo pottery the stereotyped product that it is. The techniques that have been discontinued were too widely known to have been lost through the death of individuals. Technology is not necessarily cumulative.

Pottery is still made at the present time at the following villages: Santa Clara, San Ildefonso, Sia, Santa Ana, Santo Domingo, Cochiti and Isleta on the Rio Grande; Acoma and Laguna, with their farming villages, in the central region; Zuni; and the First Mesa of Tusayan. The art is near extinction at Santa Clara, Sia, Santa Ana and Laguna; it has degenerated to the production of cheap souvenirs for tourists at Cochiti, Santo Domingo and Isleta. Pottery making is an important and profitable industry at San Ildefonso, Acoma and on the First Mesa. But it is especially at Acoma and Zuni that pottery is made primarily for household use within the village. It is therefore these villages which best represent aboriginal conditions. Most of the field work for the present study has been done at Zuni, although the stagnation and inferiority of the art there has made it advisable to include surveys of villages where commercial success has stimulated new and interesting developments.[2]

[2] In 1924 the following prices for pottery prevailed at various pueblos:

Zuni. Pottery is not ordinarily made for sale. However, a new or slightly used water jar, twelve inches high, brings the owner two or three dollars. Pottery that has been traded against credit or pawned with storekeepers is sometimes sold cheaper than this, which tends to depress the general level of prices. Large prices are asked for old and rare pieces; but the owner, if temporarily pressed for money, will not refuse offers of less.

Laguna. The principal trade is in small pieces which are sold on the road to automobile tourists, and bring the maker from fifteen to fifty cents each.

Acoma. A large water jar brings about $1.50; small pieces twenty-five to fifty cents, when sold direct to tourists; prices are probably lower for traders.

Hopi. It is impossible to state what a potter receives. The method of marketing operates very unfavorably to the potter. The villages are very remote from the market; consequently the whole output is disposed of to Tom Pavatea, the local trader, in return for credit at the store. A woman will bring in her output of two weeks, consisting of some fifty pieces of various sizes. She has an outstanding debt at the store, and the value of the pottery is used to reduce this debt. The woman has no clear conception of what she receives for her work; and Tom is reticent on this subject. Tom gets for a water jar by Nampeyo two to five dollars, depending on the size, — the five dollar size being exceptionally large for any place. A twelve inch bowl by Nampeyo, seventy-five cents. The work of other potters is cheaper. Small pieces bring from fifteen to fifty cents each. Higher prices prevail on the mesa, potters realizing the extent to which they can fleece the unwary purchaser.

San Ildefonso. Pottery is marketed on the same basis as artistic products among ourselves. Prices are conditioned by quality of craftsmanship and the fame of the maker. The work of the most famous potters is handled on a strictly commission basis by Santa Fé traders, — the only case of this kind of trading in Indian products with which the writer is familiar. A small bowl of decorated black ware by Maria Martinez brings from three to six dollars. Large and unusual pieces, such as prayer-meal bowls, vases, bring up to twelve dollars. Other potters get less for their work. A small globular bowl, six inches in diameter, by Tonita Roybal, can be purchased for three dollars; a flat bowl twelve inches in diameter, for the same price. Prices at the village are slightly lower.

Santo Domingo. A fourteen inch bowl by Monica Silva, decorated black ware, $1.50; a full size water jar in polychrome, $1 to $1.50.

II

TECHNIQUE AND FORM

The potters' wheel, or other mechanical devices for the shaping of pottery, was never used in pre-Columbian America and has not been adopted since the conquest. As a result, all pottery is still made by coiling technique. Very small pieces are made by hollowing out a single lump of clay, but larger vessels are built up by adding narrow rounds of clay to a base set in a mold. When the vessel has been built to the proper height, the shaping and thinning of the walls is accomplished by working from within with a gourd scraper. The technique employed at San Ildefonso, which is typical of the whole area, has already been adequately described.[1]

At Zuni, clay for pottery is secured at a considerable distance from the village from a place on the top of Corn Mountain where a dark gray shale abounds. The trail to this place is steep and difficult, and a journey after pottery clay is always something of an undertaking, accompanied by religious rites.[2] After the clay is brought in, it is crumbled, cleaned, spread out to dry for a day or two before it is ready for use. The tempering material is pulverized potsherds. Fragments of broken household pottery or sherds from neighboring ruins are ground to a fine powder on the metate and mixed with the fresh clay. Potters have no idea whatever of the proportions of tempering they use in the clay. In mixing the paste, they are guided entirely by their tactile sense. Doubtless experience has taught them that for a given pile of clay a certain bowl full of ground sherds will make a paste of proper consistency. The surety with which they mix the paste without having to stop in the midst to grind more sherds, or fetch more clay, shows that they are guided by some such sense of quantitative relations; but certainly they are quite unconscious of it, and unable to say when asked whether they use equal amounts of clay and tempering, or if not, what proportions prevail. One woman at Acoma gave very glibly the following ratio: two cups of tempering to each cup of clay. This ratio seems impossible; I never saw this woman mixing clay, so I seriously question the evidence. It seems, rather, merely additional proof of how foreign it is to native potters to think of the consistency of the paste in quantitative, rather than sensational terms. This is even more true of mixing with water, the next stage in the preparation of the paste. They have no sense whatever of quantitative relations of liquid and solid ingredients. As a matter of fact, it would be practically impossible to arrive inductively at any rule for the ratio of water to solids; this depends on the rapidity with which the clay is worked, since in this arid climate, evaporation must constantly be compensated for. The clay is mixed on a board or cloth spread on the floor. Kneading is a laborious task. The process of cleaning is continued as the clay is mixed, all gritty particles being removed as the soft paste is worked between the fingers.

The texture of the clay is the surest means of determining the provenience of any vessel where there is reason to suspect intertribal borrowing in design. At Laguna, for instance, I saw a pot with typical Zuni decoration and quite unlike any domestic product. However, the texture of the material established with-

[1] Guthe.
[2] M. Stevenson, 1904, p. 374.

[6]

out question that the pot was not an import, but had been made at Laguna in conscious imitation of Zuni style. Inquiries concerning the history of the vessel finally resulted in verification of this guess.

The finest ware is made at Acoma. The paste is light in color, very fine in texture, and very hard; the surfaces are extraordinarily smooth, the walls of almost egg-shell thinness. In spite of the fineness and lightness of the material, the vessels are strong and watertight. From all practical standpoints, Acoma ware is unquestionably the best pueblo product. Laguna ware of a few years back is very similar, but somewhat heavier. Weight is a better criterion than design in distinguishing Acoma and Laguna pots.

Zuni pottery is a good, serviceable ware, but heavy and coarse. The walls of the vessels are moderately thick, though not so thick as Hopi, the surfaces, where not slipped, are rather rough, the vessels are heavy, a great disadvantage where they must be carried considerable distances. Porousness is regarded as an advantage in keeping water cool in a warm climate. The paste is a dark brownish gray.

San Ildefonso ware is also heavy. It is smoother in texture than Zuni, and is hard and strong. The walls are thick, considering the size of the vessels. But the greatest weakness of San Ildefonso pottery is that it is not watertight. The beautiful black surface which constitutes the greatest charm of the ware becomes dull and streaked as soon as the vessel is filled with water, and no rubbing or polishing or greasing will ever restore it. Although beautiful, the ware from a technical point of view is worthless.

Even worse is the modern Hopi ware. The walls of the vessels are thick, the paste soft and coarse. A smooth surface is obtained by polishing, but it becomes scratched and flaked at the least friction. The vessels are very fragile, frequently they crumble when first filled with water. Whether this weakness is due to the poor quality of the clay, insufficient tempering, or underfiring, I do not know. Certainly the ware is utterly worthless.

Details of texture are characteristic for each village. The types are definitely localized, and, except for Hopi, show little variation within the local group. Although all Hopi pottery is relatively thick and coarse in texture, it is frequently possible to get pieces that will stand up under reasonable usage. It will never, however, give as good service as a Zuni or Acoma pot. The weakness of the surface finish of San Ildefonso pottery is as characteristic as its black color. It is part of the ware and not due to slovenliness of individual craftsmanship. This is true also of the heaviness of Zuni pots. These factors are, as a rule, remarkably constant in each group at any one time, even if they do not remain constant for any long period of time.

In starting to mold a vessel, a lump of clay is first worked with the hands, and by hollowing this out, or pressing it flat, a cup or disc shaped base is formed, which is placed in a low mold. This is made either of the bottom of a broken pot or a saucer or pie tin filled with clay and sprinkled with sand. The base is pressed carefully into the mold, and the walls are built up by adding rounds of clay. The clay is rolled between the hands or on the floor into long thin strips which are added to the top of the vessel. The strips are usually about an inch in diameter and from two to three feet long, depending on the skill of the potter in handling the material. The strips are always placed inside the finished wall and pressed into place with the fingers. Great care must be exercised in rolling and joining so that no air spaces remain, for any cracks or spaces will cause the vessel to break during the firing. In making small vessels the walls are built up to the full height, except for the neck, before the shaping is begun. In larger vessels, preliminary shaping accompanies the building. With the exception of smoothing the outer surface, all shaping is done from the interior. The only tools used are fragments of gourd shell, pieces of different curative being used for shaping the inside and outside, and for the body and neck of the vessel. Almost all the vessels made at Zuni are large water jars which must be shaped as they are built. When built up to a point somewhat below the shoulder, the vessel is set aside for a few hours to become firm enough to support the upper walls. During this time the upper edge must be kept constantly wet. When considering native sensitivity to form, it is important to remember that the lower part of the vessel is set in its final form before the upper part is molded. The form must be clearly visualized in its entirety before the half finished vessel is set aside to dry, for after that time no corrections are possible. As with the mixing of the clay, the final form is not arrived at by a process of trial and error, — by adding a little there and taking off something here, until a satisfactory form is attained, — but, rather, the operator is guided by a very definite sense of proportion, no less rigorous because it is unconscious.

That it is wholly unconscious, I have not the slightest doubt. From no woman in any pueblo did I get any rules of proportions. At San Ildefonso certain potters are now making tall vases copied from a piece of American pottery loaned by a trader. I have seen a number of such vases, all so accurately reproduced that they might almost have been cast from the same mold. In spite of this constancy of form, when I called the attention of potters to the most obvious dimensions, for instance the ratio of base to neck, which is always 2:3, they all agreed that this was something of which they had never before thought. It is quite foreign to their methods to think of form in terms of numerical ratios. Nor are they guided by the number or size of the strips of clay used. The strips are rolled as long as can be conveniently handled, since every joining is a possible source of weakness. If the strip so made is longer than required, it is broken off; if too short, another piece is added. They do not count the strips as they work, thinking that after a certain number of rounds, it will be time to start on the neck. They have no very clear ideas of how many strips are used.[3] Not only are they not guided

by any definite quantitative concepts in the creation of their forms, they are even unconscious of the outstanding characteristics of the vessels when finished. The most general principles I could elicit were, "It must be even all around, not larger on one side than another," (this from all potters, without a single exception), the neck must not be too long; the mouth must not be too small. But of definite ratios between height and diameter, or between total height and height of shoulder, not to mention more subtle features, they seemed wholly unconscious, and this in spite of the fact that the finished vessels are ordinarily carefully measured for the adjustment of the design. But this must by no means be taken as implying that native potters are not extremely sensitive to problems of form; this sensitivity, and the very definite sense of proportion, are shown both in the uniformity of vessels from any one village and in the distinctly critical attitude towards any deviation from the accepted forms.

The impression of uniformity in the vessels of any village is based on rather elusive traits. It is, in one sense, more apparent than real. Gross measurements on a large number of vessels show a considerable range of variation both in the actual dimensions and the ratios between them.[4] The general outlines of water jars of Acoma and Zuni are the same. They have narrow bases, swelling out gradually until the greatest circumference is reached at about three-fifths of the height. The vessel is then constricted to form the neck, the diameter of the rim being about half the greatest diameter of the body. In Zuni jars the total height is about three-fourths of the greatest diameter; Acoma jars are a trifle higher. The greater number of water jars range from 16 to 29 inches in height, and from 18 to 36 inches in diameter. The capacity is

[3] This agrees with observation of Hopi coiled baskets. A count of stitches forming corresponding parts of patterns shows no agreement. The checkered rim of a placque was blocked off into regular squares which contained anywheres from 5 to 11 stitches each.

[4] Professor Boas reports a similar experience in analysis of painted and carved wooden boxes from the Northwest Coast. Distinction of form is not based on direct ratios, or on any principles of dynamic symmetry.

PLATE I

OUTLINES OF TYPICAL PUEBLO VESSELS

a-d, San Ildefonso; e, Hopi; f, Zuni; g, Hopi; h, Zuni; i, Acoma

[9]

from 4 to 6 gallons. These figures are, of course, but an approximation.

In spite of the general agreement in form of Acoma and Zuni jars, the two types can easily be distinguished. The outlines of Acoma jars are smoother; they show a single unbroken curve from base to rim. At Zuni there is a definite break between neck and body, and another between body and base. The lower break is at the point where the vessel emerges from the mold, and is caused by the worker pushing the sides of the vessel out over the mold, or by the clay settling as it dries. This roughness is smoothed out in the finishing of vessels at other pueblos; at Zuni, however, it is retained as a significant part of the structure, and is recognized in the decoration. This ridge marks the boundary between the base, which is left unslipped, and the body, which is slipped in white and decorated. (See Pl. I, h, i.)

The break between body and neck also marks the line between two distinct decorative fields. This break, which occurs some distance above the point of greatest girth, is very noticeable on all Zuni jars, and is marked with a heavy black line.[5] It is interesting to note that at Acoma where there is no break in the curve of the vessel, the whole surface is treated as a single decorative field.

I have taken very few measurements on bowls. The characteristic Zuni bowl is an almost perfect half sphere, about 12 to 15 inches in diameter. There is a slight constriction a few inches below the rim, forming a neck similar to that on jars. It is particularly marked on the interior, and here is recognized in laying on the pattern. In some bowls the constriction is lower, and more marked, and the rim decidedly flaring. Bowls are not at present made at Acoma.

The Hopi water jar is low and wide-spreading, — the total height being slightly less than two-thirds of the diameter. The shoulder is high and the mouth very small, with the result that the upper part of the vessel is nearly flat. (See Pl. I, g.) This is the ancient Sikyatki form, one that at one time had a wide distribution. It was once the typical form

in the Zuni valley, where it gradually gave way to the present type. This form is especially well adapted for carrying water long distances over steep, rough trails, as is necessary in the Hopi country. The low flat vessel is more easily balanced on the head than higher forms; the small mouth prevents spilling. However tempting this theory is as an explanation of development of this peculiar form in Tusayan, it is without foundation in fact. In ancient times this type of vessel was developed when the Hopi villages were situated in valleys, and it flourished at the same time in the Zuni valley. During the nineteenth century the typical Hopi water jar was an unwieldy globular affair, much clumsier than that now made at Zuni. Acoma, a mesa village, where conditions are similar to those of the Hopi country, favors high large-mouthed jars.

Although water jars are still made at First Mesa, the characteristic Hopi form is the small bowl, originally intended for serving food. In early days these were ten inches in diameter, but now the same type of vessel is made in all sizes, even as small as five inches. These bowls are very shallow with curved bases and slightly incurved rims.

At San Ildefonso a great variety of small forms are made. The commonest type is a shallow bowl, somewhat like the Hopi bowl, with flat bases and a more definitely incurved rim. Several kinds of deep bowls are made, — three very popular forms are shown in Plate I, a-c. Many other forms are also made, covered boxes, both rectangular and cylindrical, plates, high vases, even candlesticks. These are copied from articles of American manufacture, and for the white trade. They have not been made for a long enough period to have become assimilated to the native pottery complex. When native potters begin to experiment with these forms, it will be interesting to see what they do with them. But at the present time they have no interest for us as forms, although from the standpoint of design they present one of the most interesting groups with which we have to deal.[6]

From this brief survey we see that form, in

5 See p. 13.

6 See p. 46.

spite of general similarities over the whole area, is as definitely stylized for each particular village as is design. The differences between a Zuni and Acoma water jar are subtle, yet they are not unrecognized by native potters. A Zuni potter when shown a photograph of an Acoma pot will immediately remark that she does not like the shape; the neck is "funny." She cannot formulate her criticism more definitely than that, but then neither could many more sophisticated persons. With us, also, a thing offends when it violates a principle of whose very existence we are unaware.

Potters who have no constructive suggestions in regard to proportions are very quick indeed to note and comment upon an irregular rim or an asymmetrical body. These points are especially emphasized in instruction also. There is no potter whom I interviewed who did not mention specifically the need of care in these matters of modelling. For them all problems of form of which they are conscious are semi-technical, the attainment of perfection within imposed limits. The creative process itself lies deeper than consciousness.

Probably the most laborious part of the whole process of pottery making is the surface finishing. When the vessel is thoroughly dry, the rough finishing begins. The whole surface is moistened and scraped, inside and out, with a knife, the top of a baking powder tin, or a rough stone. All roughness is worn down. It is at this point that the ridge formed at the top of the mold is eliminated. The walls are further thinned by this process, and the rim is made smooth and regular. This rough finishing is done very hurriedly and carelessly at Zuni, and as a result Zuni jars show all kinds of irregularities of surface, of which the ridge at the top of the mold is the most characteristic. Great care is lavished on this process at other places. If at this point in the manufacture any imperfections of structure are noted, such as cracks, air bubbles or pieces of gritty material embedded in clay, any one of which would cause the pot to break

during the firing, the vessel is destroyed and the clay used over again. Cooking pots, which are neither polished nor painted, are ready for the fire after the rough finishing. Cooking pots, however, are practically never made any more.

When all roughness of contour has been corrected, the real process of finishing begins. First the slip is applied to all surfaces to be thus treated. At Zuni, only the upper part of jars is slipped, that is, the part above the mold. Elsewhere jars are slipped over their whole outer surface. At Zuni bowls are slipped on the inside and the upper part of the outside; Hopi bowls are slipped inside and out; San Ildefonso bowls on the outside only. Everywhere decoration is applied to slipped surfaces only; at Zuni all slipped surfaces are decorated.

The slip is a thin solution of very fine clay containing no tempering. It is applied to the surface evenly with a smooth cloth. Usually three or four coatings are applied. The color of the slip varies at different pueblos. At Zuni, Acoma, and Laguna it is chalky white. The bases of Laguna and Acoma pots, corresponding to the unslipped portion of Zuni jars are slipped with bright orange-red. Hopi pots are slipped with the same clay that forms the paste. This is clear, light gray before it is fired, but turns yellow during the firing, shading from pale ivory to deep buff, tinged with rose. This mottled effect, due to irregular firing, is one of the chief beauties of the ware. It is less marked in the original Sikyatki ware which is more evenly fired. A few pieces of pottery are slipped in red or in white. San Ildefonso pots are slipped in bright red, which, if the fire is smothered at the right moment, turns to a deep lustrous black. The color of the slip shows little variation within any group. Among the Hopi the color varies considerably in different pieces by the same maker, and even in the same piece. This variability in color is quite characteristic of the material, and is not the result of deliberate choice. It is a matter of chance whether or not a pot is light or dark or mottled. But at Zuni and Acoma there is no variation from the dead white, nor at San Ildefonso from the clear black or red.

Polishing is begun while the last coating of the slip is still damp. The polish is attained by rubbing the surface lightly with a very smooth stone. Polishing stones are concretions of various kinds which women pick up wherever they find them. The use of the polishing stone requires very great skill; just the right amount of pressure must be exerted to obtain a high polish without scratching or pebbling the surface. By careful polishing a very smooth and even glossy surface is obtained. The glossiness is generally lost during the firing. At San Ildefonso, however, the polish is used as the chief source of ornament. Here the polishing is done with even greater care than is exercised in other places. When a very high polish has been secured by the use of the stone, the surface is rubbed with a greasy rag. The whole process of finishing is done with the most meticulous care. If a single scratch or irregularity is observed, a fresh coating of clay is applied and the whole process is repeated. Potters everywhere are very emphatic about the need for care at this point in the manufacture.

Surface finish is extremely variable. At San Ildefonso differences in surface finish are more characteristic of the work of certain individuals than peculiarities of form or design. Even at Zuni where surface finish is by no means so important, differences are conspicuous. Although for the most part a smooth surface is all that is required, some vessels show a very acceptable polish. Here, too, it is a matter of individual variation, exceptional surface finish being characteristic of the work of certain potters. Highly polished pieces are more common among old collections. Apparently at one time surface finish received more attention than it does at present. This is true also of Acoma and Hopi. Old pieces are more highly polished than contemporary products.

When the polishing is finished, the vessel is ready to receive the design. Except at Santa Clara, where some undecorated black pottery is still made, all pueblo pottery of the present day is decorated with painting or similar types of ornament. It is this part of the art which shows the greatest local and individual variation, and thus provides the most fruitful field of inquiry.

III

THE PRINCIPLES OF DESIGN

It is necessary at this point to leave our potter with her vessel ready for decoration in order to analyze more objectively the various decorative types represented within the field of this study. Certain principles of design may be found to underly each type, and it is well to have these clearly in mind before trying to discover the way that the individual potter operates within the limits of the style or escapes from it. For this reason it is the purpose of the following pages to formulate general principles of design rather than to describe individual pieces or analyze statistically the ceramic product of any village.

Zuni

The slipped surface of Zuni jars is divided into two contiguous zones of decoration, separated from one another by the constriction of the neck, to which we have already referred. The area is continuous, and the break very slight, yet there is no doubt that we are dealing with two, rather than one, decorative problem. The treatment of the two fields is entirely different. Their separateness is reflected in native terminology. The upper field is called the "neck" (sometimes the "lips," although the latter term is generally used only for the rim proper), and the lower and larger field, the "stomach." This terminology reflects also native recognition of the structural character of the two fields. The "neck" is generally about one palm's breadth wide, approximately one-fourth of the whole decorated surface, and equal to the undecorated zone at the base. The division into two fields is characteristic not only of water jars but of bowls as well, an equivalent portion being set off from the main field on the interior of all bowls.

The first bit of decoration that goes on any Zuni jar or bowl is the heavy line that marks the division between neck and body. This is the line that is always left unjoined and about which cling so many superstitions. All potters agreed that this line is an essential, indeed, the most important part of the design, confusing in their statements its decorative and symbolic functions. Its symbolic character will be discussed in another place.[1] Whatever the cause, the emphasis which has been placed by Zuni potters on this obviously structural line has had an important influence in shaping the character of Zuni decoration.

All the potters whom I interviewed were explicit in their statements that this line is indispensable; nevertheless, even so fixed a rule is not without exception. Of rare occurrence is a type of very shallow bowl which has no border. I have seen but one example of this type, a bowl of great age, a family heirloom used for ceremonial purposes; and this shows evidence of the rim having been broken off and ground down. The type, however, is recognized in native terminology. I also saw one jar which did not show the traditional division into neck and body. The pattern on this jar is very untypical in many ways. It may be significant that both the bowl and the jar which deviated from the general pattern belonged to the same woman, although not both had been made by her. The bowl had been made by her grandmother when she was a little girl, and had been in the family ever since.

[1] See p. 69.

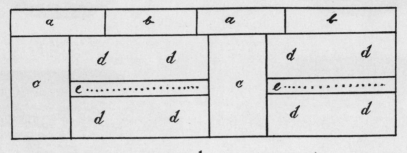

a

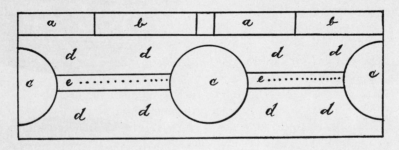

b

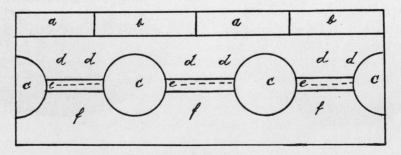

c

d

PLATE II
DESIGN ARRANGEMENTS ON ZUNI JARS, AMNH
[14]

a

b

c

d

e

f

PLATE III

Modern Zuni water jars

a, AMNH; b, author's collection; c-f, USNM

[15]

The water-jar. A Zuni artist sums up the general method of decorating a water jar as follows:

First I paint the stomach and then I paint the lips. I always use different designs on the lips and the stomach. You do not have to use the same number of designs on the lips as you use on the body.

Examination of specimens of Zuni pottery bears out these statements. The neck and the body are always differently decorated. Except for the fact that a certain harmony is preserved in the selection of patterns for neck and body, the two fields are wholly unrelated. There is no attempt to use the same number of designs on neck and body, but on the other hand, there does not seem to be any deliberate striving for a decorative effect by making the numbers of designs unequal. It seems to be a matter of chance whether the numerical division is the same or different. Where the same number of designs are used in both fields, no attempt is made to make the lines of division coincide.

The decoration of the neck is always a simple panelled band. In painting, the band is first blocked off into equal rectangular, or more accurately, trapezoidal spaces, and one decorative motif is allotted to each space. The arrangement most favored at the present time is the alternation of two different designs, using in all four, six or occasionally eight units. On small jars this alternating arrangement is frequently replaced by the repetition of a single motif, but the same characteristic division into rectangular spaces separated by heavy lines is adhered to. This simpler scheme was formerly used also on larger jars. Older jars also show borders of continuous or interlocking spirals, modified frets, disconnected double spirals, and other patterns now wholly obsolete. The present preferred designs for the neck are Nos. 76 and 77, and 79 A and B.[2] Two fundamentally different types of composition are possible on the body of the water jar. These might be called simple and composite arrangements. In what I have called the simple arrangement the field is

² Numbers refer to the numbered series of Zuni designs in Appendix I.

treated as a unit and ornamented by one motive repeated at regular intervals — see Plate III a, e. Subsidiary designs may be introduced between the main designs, especially in the upper and larger portion of the jar, but their function is merely that of fillers. It is an important characteristic of Zuni decoration that all designs are born to a certain station in life. A neck design can never rise to the dignity of a stomach design, and no stomach design would demean itself to the extent of adorning a neck. In the same way the correct connections of each stomach design are fixed by taste. Certain designs are invariably used in simple, others in composite arrangement. The more important designs that take the simple arrangement are all the "cloud-step" designs, e.g. No. 5. The number of units may be anywhere from three to nine. All artists expressed a preference for four units, but three is by far the most common number, the other numbers following in numerical sequence. As might be expected certain designs show marked preferences for certain numbers, — the design in Plate III, a, for instance, being invariably used in tripartite arrangement. In pottery of the last century, alternating units were occasionally used on the body of jars, but this arrangement has since become obsolete.

By far the more characteristic Zuni style is the composite arrangement, which admits considerable variation. Some of the more usual forms are shown in Pl. II, b-d; Pl. III, b-d, f. The one thing common to all these arrangements is the unequal division of the field. The surface is first divided vertically into large and small areas, the larger sections being further subdivided into two or three unequal horizontal bands. The upper and lower bands are generally of equal width, with a very much narrower band between. These fields are all clearly marked off one from the other by the same heavy black lines that are used on the neck and between neck and body. The whole surface thus divided presents a combination of vertical and horizontal fields, the effect being prevailingly horizontal. The vertical panel is frequently replaced by a cir-

a

b

c

d

e

f

PLATE IV

OLD ZUNI JARS, ABOUT 1875, USNM

[17]

cular medallion, in which case the horizontal theme is still further emphasized. Where vertical panels are used the division is always into two panels and two horizontal sections. Either two or three medallions may be used. All potters expressed a preference for two, but three seems to be equally common in their work.

In each of the vertical panels a single design is used. One motif is twice repeated in each of the upper horizontal fields. The same unit may also be used twice in each of the lower fields, but, owing to the shape of the vessel, this field is so much smaller than the upper one that a different design is frequently chosen. For the narrow strip a continuous band is used, or a single unit repeated to fill.

For each of these four fields, one or several designs may be chosen, but the position in which any one design may be used is absolutely fixed. For instance, the deer design (Nos. 10, 11), or any one of the large spiral designs (Nos. 12 and 13) may be used in the horizontal fields, but neither of these is ever used in any other position. In the same way several designs are available for the vertical panel (Nos. 16-19), and still others for the narrow bands dividing the upper and lower fields (Nos. 20-23).

I found in use in Zuni two jars which do not fall into either of the foregoing classifications, which may be regarded as aberrant types. The first was the jar already alluded to, which does not show the characteristic Zuni division into neck and body. It shows the diagonal arrangement that is so characteristic of Acoma, and is undoubtedly a loan design, although unquestionably of Zuni manufacture. The other jar was divided into two horizontal fields of equal width, the upper containing nine designs and fillers, the lower band containing seven designs. This is a type of arrangement that was once fairly common.

The foregoing analysis is applicable only to contemporary products. On older pots greater freedom in arrangement is noticeable, — all of the above-mentioned types being represented, as well as others. The following types are commonly found:

1. Alternating units, generally four in all. (Pl. IV, a).

2. Horizontal division into two approximately equal bands, sometimes with a narrower band between. (Pl. IV, b.)

3. Vertical division into unequal sections, similar to the modern composite treatment without the horizontal banding. (Pl. IV, e.)[3]

In composite arrangements there is greater freedom of number, — three or even four vertical panels being used. Occasionally two panels and two medallions are used. There is, moreover, a greater freedom in the use of decorative motives. Spirals, for example, are used alone in simple arrangement (Pl. V, a), and deer are used in the narrow band. Neither of these arrangements would be favorably regarded at the present time. Motives, however, are not used with absolute freedom. Although the association is not so fixed as at present, certain designs appear more frequently in certain combinations, — this greater frequency always corresponding with the present accepted arrangement. The possible causes of the greater rigidity of style at the present time will be discussed in another place.

Bowls. Bowls are decorated both on their inner and outer surfaces. The outer field is a continuous band around the rim, about a span deep. For this band one design (No. 60) is used almost universally. Other borders used rarely in this position are sketched in Nos. 59-65.

As we have already noted, the interior is divided into two fields, — a central circular field, and a border, which in a large bowl is four finger widths deep. The border is always treated continuously, several designs being available for this position. Typical border designs are shown in Nos. 66-74.

The central field of the bowl exhibits the greatest diversity of design to be seen anywhere in Zuni decorative art. (See Pl. VI, for typical arrangements.) The following types may be distinguished:

1. A radiating design repeated three to five times. Pl. VI, a.

[3] A few examples of each of the two last types were seen at Zuni in 1928.

a

b

PLATE V

Old Zuni jars, 1850-1875, USNM

2. Division into three or four similar pie slice fields, clearly marked off. Pl. VI, b.

3. Alternating designs in pairs, so arranged that similar designs occupy opposite quarters of the field, generally without clearly marked division. (Pl. VI, c, Pl. VII, b.)

4. A composition similar to 3, but with the parts interlocked to form a single design.

5. A single radiating design — the swastika, — a very rare arrangement, and so far as I was able to discover, now obsolete. A single old bowl with this design was still in use in Zuni in 1925.

Of these types, 3 seems to be the preferred arrangement at the present time. Apparently there is no restriction in the use of designs on bowls, such as prevails in the decoration of water jars. All designs are used with the greatest freedom, the most usual arrangement being triangular units connected by graceful scrolls (Pl. VII, b.)

This analysis of the decoration of bowls is regretably sketchy because the material is very meager. The bowl is practically extinct at Zuni. The medium-sized food bowl is no longer seen, and its place has been taken by platters and soup plates of white manufacture. The large mixing bowls are still used, but so far as I was able to see, they are not being replaced when broken. The American dish-pan has evidently come to stay. Bowls have always shown greater variability. Exact duplication in bowls is exceedingly rare; the same thing most decidedly cannot be said of water jars. For this reason it is especially deplorable that the material is so scanty.

One of the most important factors in determining the character of Zuni decorative style is the strict limitation of the number of designs admissible on any vessel. It is quite clear in the minds of all artists that the number of designs is fixed, and that the patterns selected must be enlarged or reduced to a size suitable for the particular surface to be decorated. Along with this goes a very marked aversion to overcrowding. This is so very characteristic, that I shall quote a few comments of informants:

I do not like to have the whole jar covered with paint. If I use large designs, I leave large spaces between, so that it won't look dirty.

There should be a good deal of white showing. If you put on too many small designs, the jar is too black and that is not nice. I do not use too much black because it makes the jar dirty looking.

If there is room, I sometimes use four big designs on a large jar. If the jar is very large, I use larger designs. I never use more than four. . . . I like a lot of white showing.

All the potters had very decided number preferences, and on these they were pretty well agreed. Expressed preferences were as follows: for simple designs, four was considered best, three also is very good, six is permissible, five is not good, and more than six is very bad; for composite designs, a two part arrangement is to be preferred to three part, more than three should not be used. An examination of pottery, however, shows that actual numerical preferences are not the ones expressed. In simple arrangements anything from three to nine may be used, the number depending in a large measure on the particular pattern selected. For instance, the design on the jar in Pl. III, a, is invariably used in threes. For other patterns the rule is not so fixed, — No. 5 (also shown in Pl. III, e), for instance, has been observed from four to seven times. Because of the great popularity of the design shown in Pl. III, a, which appears oftener than any other pattern of this type, an actual count of vessels shows three designs appearing oftener than any other number, — with four as a bad second, and the other numbers following consecutively. The arrangement of composite designs also shows certain peculiarities in the use of number. Where vertical panels are used, a two-part division is almost invariable, but where medallions are used instead, examples seem to be fairly evenly distributed between two and three part divisions.

In the decoration of bowls a balanced design of two or four units is exceedingly common, but three part arrangements are by no means unknown. In fact, there seems to be the requisite number for certain designs, partic-

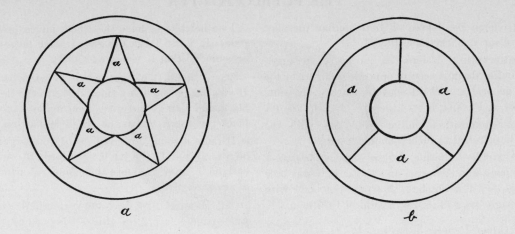

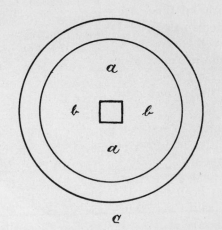

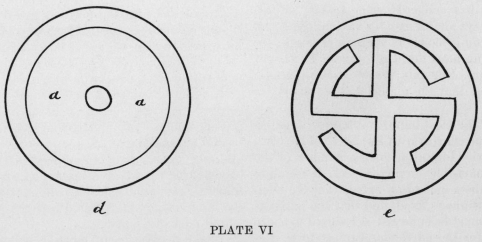

PLATE VI

DESIGN ARRANGEMENTS ON ZUNI BOWLS

a-d, AMNH; e, author's collection

a

b

c

PLATE VII

MODERN ZUNI BOWLS, USNM

ularly the large spiral designs which are so common in the decoration of bowls.

I find this discrepancy between expressed preference and actual usage exceedingly interesting in view of other phases of Zuni life. The importance of the number four in custom and belief is very marked. Furthermore, the literary pattern is always four, and, in a very large measure, the ceremonial pattern. It is therefore perfectly fitting and logical that Zuni artists in talking of their painting should always express a preference for the number four. But apparently at the moment of execution a purely esthetic factor intervenes in the feeling for decorative form, and substitutes the number three for the expected four.

The Zuni artist recognizes that her designs can be analyzed into smaller units. The ease with which these can be isolated is evidenced by the collection of ninety-four design sketches shown in Plates XXI-XXXII, Appendix I, all drawn for me on paper by one of the oldest and best informed Zuni potters.

I reproduce the collection precisely as it was made, since it represents better than any comments the extent and limitations of native analysis. These are not design elements in any sense that would satisfy a sophisticated analyst of design. They are patterns adapted to use on special parts of vessels. Native analysis goes no further. These are the psychological elements, although they might be reduced to a very much smaller number of structural elements.

According to the artist's statements, this collection represents her complete stock of patterns. Nevertheless, despite her earnest efforts, the collection is not quite complete and I have observed a number of other designs on her pottery. Twenty-four of these designs, have been described as "old," — that is, no longer in use. In a very cursory examination of the large quantity of pottery collected in Zuni in 1879-1880, and now in the United States National Museum at Washington, I was able to find a great many of these obsolete designs, most of them being represented by several examples. The identification

was by no means exhaustive, but it was sufficient to indicate that most of these designs were generally known and used within the lifetime of the woman who drew them. Making allowances for omission of a considerable number of well known obsolete designs, which, of course, would be greater than current designs, we see that what we might call the design vocabulary of the Zuni potter has considerable range and variety. If any attempt were made to collect all known Zuni designs in use within the period mentioned, the collection would be several times multiplied.

The designs fall readily into two classes, sacred and secular. The cleavage between household and ceremonial objects in regard to form and decoration is so complete that it is difficult to believe that two such different ceramic types belong to the same age and the same people. The usual form of the prayer-meal bowl is a small basket-shaped vessel, with terraced rim and a handle across the top. (Pl. VIII, d.) It is slipped with white, inside and out. The square cut rim is painted black, and a narrow black stripe runs just below the edge. The bowl is decorated inside and out with any or all of the following designs: the serpent (No. 2); the frog; the tadpole, and the dragonfly (No. 1). These are all representative designs of the simplest type, entirely uninfluenced by the requisites of a decorative style. The designs are painted directly on the white background without reference to one another; the carefully integrated structure that characterizes the household pottery is wholly lacking. The serpent design is an accurate representation of the Kolowisi fetish, a very important ceremonial possession, a copy of which is in the United States National Museum. The frog and the tadpole are also crudely naturalistic. The dragonfly is slightly stylized, a rather impressionistic picture of a dragonfly. The designs are crudely conceived and crudely executed. These same characteristics appear also in the two pottery drums in Pl. IX. These drums are not strictly modern products, but exactly the same paintings are still used on the walls of certain ceremonial rooms in

Zuni. From the crude and hasty workmanship of all these sacred paintings, we may infer that the purpose of the artist is to depict rather than to adorn, and that esthetic standards have had very little to do with the development of these patterns. This, of course, is characteristic of religious art in other places.[4] The greater realism of religious art is also shown in the use of modelling on the sacred meal bowls, a technique which has entirely disappeared from the secular art. The symbolic step design which is always painted on household articles is invariably modelled along the rim of prayer-meal bowls.

Of the secular designs, only two approach the realism of the ceremonial patterns. These are the deer (Nos. 10, 11), and the bird (No. 20). The deer, which has slipped over from ceremonial painting, becomes stylized through the graceful scroll work which invariably surrounds it, and which makes of it a pattern rather than a picture. The bird appears in several variants of the pattern shown here. Long graceful tails are rather more common than the short stubby one here used. The birds also show the influence of style. The way in which they are used, — always in narrow, clearly defined borders, — adds to the conventional effect. The butterfly and dragonfly patterns (Nos. 36, 53, 84) are all highly stylized. The single plant form, the medallion which goes by the name of sun-flower (No. 9), is also conventionalized.

The only other representative designs now in use are the feather designs. These are represented in this collection by Nos. 60 and 79 A. These patterns must not by any means be considered highly conventionalized birds, in which the bird form has been lost and the feathers retained as a symbol. If they symbolize anything, it certainly is not birds. The ceremonial importance of feathers is very great. These feather patterns are not highly symbolic birds, but very slightly conventionalized prayer-sticks. No. 79 A in particular is a not inaccurate representation of the stick for the dead, which has four feathers turned

inwards, fastened close together to the stick, with a fifth, a soft duck feather, turned outwards, fastened a little below the other four.[5]

A striking feature of this series of Zuni designs is the complete absence, with a single exception, of all plant forms, or of patterns that appear to be derived from plant forms. Some of the small spiral patterns go by the name of "flowers," and these trailing arrangements may, perhaps, have been suggested by the form of the squash vine, but the relationship surely is not very close. There is no representation of topographical features, houses or other articles of human manufacture.

This brief enumeration completes the list of representative designs. They are few in number, but their constant use makes them a most important group. These patterns are all of the very recent origin. Certainly they cannot claim equal antiquity with the spiral and the cloud-step patterns. Naturalistic designs are not found in the most recent deposits of Hawikuh.[6] Certainly the highly conventionalized animal and bird forms of Hawikuh polychrome ware cannot be regarded as ancestral. The representative designs, especially the deer, are used in great number and with the greatest freedom on the pottery of the 70's. The stylistic features of the present designs, such as the inevitable deer's "house" were less pronounced at that time, and I venture to conclude that these designs were newly developed in that period, and had not yet become incorporated into the prevailingly geometric style.

This brings us to a consideration of the geometrical patterns which constitute the greater part of the present collection. We must not be misled into considering these patterns representative merely because they bear the names of objects, or are so interpreted.[7]

---

[4] Boas discusses this characteristic of the religious art of another area in an interesting paper. Boas, 1903.

[5] For a discussion of the symbolism of feather designs, see p. 69.

[6] Hodge, 1924.

[7] The question might be asked whether these numerous "steps" designs which are inevitably interpreted as clouds are not representative designs. I am fully convinced that this is not the case. See pp. 53, 69.

a

b

c

d

PLATE VIII

Prayer-meal bowls

a, San Ildefonso, AMNH; b-d Zuni, USNM

PLATE IX

POTTERY DRUMS FROM ZUNI, USNM

[26]

One of the important groups of geometric designs are the so-called "steps" designs. These patterns are all fairly compact, with large surfaces treated with hatching and outlined with heavier black lines, and they are in all probability derived from the ancient fret patterns. Certainly No. 5 is so derived. Reduced to its simplest outlines, its relationship to the interlocking fret of the black-on-white period is unmistakable. A similar pattern has been observed on the inner surface of a bowl. In its present form it shows decided resemblance to the black and white patterns of the Upper Gila. Plate III, a, and No. 46 are variants of the same pattern, — No. 46 being an aberrent form, and Pl. III, a, being a very common design. I am at a loss to account for the irregular form of this design, and especially for the presence of the spiral. It is undoubtedly related to the other spiral designs, especially to No. 79, but how it came to be combined with the steps remains a mystery. The pattern is undoubtedly related to those shown in Pl. IV, f, Pl. V, b. The age of the pot, Pl. V, b, can only be guessed, but undoubtedly it is very ancient. In this design greater prominence is given to the spiral.

More important even than the steps patterns are the spirals, which are represented in great numbers and great variety. The more important forms of the spiral are the following:

1. The large spiral, with two large triangular appendages (Nos. 12, 13), fitted together in pairs to cover the horizontal fields of water jars, or in threes in the interior of bowls.
2. The spiral with hatching (No. 79), which also has appendages, in particular two small triangles, separated by a small rectangular figure.
3. The spiral with the steps.
4. Interlocking spiral band (Nos. 21, 22).
5. The small spiral, either with or without appendages, used singly or joined together in endless variety, as fillers in connection with many designs.

The peculiar appendages which characterize types 2 and 3 above, and which seem to have no relation to the design, and the frequent use of eye forms in both these types, may indicate that the spiral at one stage in its development was representative in character, and possibly associated with Kolowisi, the plumed serpent. The peculiar form of the design on Pl. IV, f, which was once quite common but which is now obsolete, lends some support to the theory that we are here dealing with a highly conventionalized serpent motif. However, this is hypothetical at best.

Triangles are ordinarily used as fillers, especially around the upper portion of the bodies of pots. The surface is generally filled with hatchure, often cross hatchure. When used as fillers, the base of the triangle is placed against the upper border of the field, and the two sides are bordered with scalloped or notched figures. A triangle enclosing a white square is a common motive, and may possibly be related to the similar motive in Plains beadwork. (No. 5.) A long slender triangle with notched corners (No. 77) is one of the important neck designs. Triangular figures built entirely of curved lines are much used in the decoration of bowls, the curvature probably being due to the character of the surface.

Squares and diamonds, outlined with several parallel lines, are used in the centers of bowls. A similar diamond design is used on the necks of jars.

Circles, generally surrounded by a ring of scallops, are used in the centers of bowls. Similar circular figures are used on the vertical panels of jars, the corners of the panel being filled with a kind of square fret.

The collection includes a great variety of notched figures, the use of which remains a mystery to me. They are all now obsolete and my informant could not explain just how they were used; and a study of older pottery has failed to throw much light on them.

One characteristic of all these decorative motives which is just mentioned incidentally here, is the very marked lack of duplicating symmetry. The number of patterns that can be bisected into two identical halves can be counted on the fingers of one hand.

It is characteristic of Zuni decoration that the designs are all patterns of line rather than of surface. Many forms are presented in outline only. The moon, for instance, is always represented as a thin ring (No. 16), never as a solid circle of color. There is always a marked avoidance of surfaces executed in solid color. In the only designs in which surfaces are handled decoratively, the steps designs, fine line hatching is always used. Hatched surfaces are always outlined in heavier black lines.

Next to overcrowding, the most frequent criticism heard in Zuni is "too much paint." Plenty of clear white space, or surfaces lightly treated with fine line work, please best, and the pot in which the patterns are executed with a free use of paint is called "dirty looking." I had with me at Zuni a number of photographs of pottery from different pueblos, and I gave to my Zuni informant a photograph of Santo Domingo jars which she especially admired. When I asked her to execute a similar design for me on one of her own jars, she copied the design accurately even to the smallest details until she came to filling in the black surfaces. Then she asked me whether she might paint these differently, because she was afraid the jar would be "dirty" if she used so much black paint. She considered red as an alternative, but thought the surfaces were too large for red, and finally decided on the typical Zuni hatching, which, of course, completely destroyed the original character of the design.

Zuni decoration is essentially a black on white style. Red is used so sparingly that it does not affect the general black and white aspect. Red is used somewhat more generously on bowls, but even here the predominant color is black, and black could be substituted for all the red painting without greatly altering the character of the design. However, red and black cannot be used interchangeably. All structural lines are black. The principal designs are painted mostly in black with touches of red in certain places. The use of red for fillers is optional, but many women prefer to make these black also. Black and red fillings are never used in contiguous areas, although red fillers are outlined with black. Entire black and white pots are not unusual, and do not stand out from the general run of three color pots. The absence of red would scarcely be noticed by a casual observer.

One characteristic of the whole decorative scheme of Zuni pottery is the very marked lack of duplicating symmetry. This is noticeable in the individual patterns that make up the Zuni alphabet, very few of which can be bisected into two identical halves. To paint a bird or an animal with two heads in order to preserve the symmetry of the design would be utterly foreign to Zuni taste. This applies to the geometrical patterns as well as the representative. The "steps" designs which could so easily be made symmetrical without destroying their character are never so drawn. There seems, in fact, to be a careful avoidance of this particular type of symmetry, in spite of the fact that the parts of the design are carefully balanced. This lack of duplicating symmetry extends also to the arrangement of the motives. There is no feeling that the designs on any field must be arranged with reference to an imaginary center line. The decorative importance of this principle is most apparent in the treatment of the deer and sunflower designs. An artist trained in our traditions would certainly treat these motives differently. He would turn the two deer in each horizontal field either towards one another or away from one another, dividing the field into two halves, each of which mirrors the other, and bringing the two deer on each side of the sunflower into the same relationship with it. He would probably also open all the arches out towards the central horizontal line, instead of having all open downwards. However, the Zuni artist opens all his arches downwards, and turns all his deer with their heads to the right, which creates a strong feeling of movement and greatly emphasizes the generally horizontal feeling of the design. The same principles are applied, but with less striking effect, to the treatment of spirals. These are generally, but not always, fitted into one another without regard to their relative positions on the field. (See Pl. V, a.)

The lack in Zuni design of the particular

kind of symmetry which we expect in our own decorative art, but which is by no means common to other styles, does not mean that Zuni designs are constructed without a careful balancing of the various units. Jars are arranged with two panels balancing one another on opposite sides of the jar, with similar balancing sections between. The whole jar is symmetrically laid out, but the distinctive character comes from the rythmical, rather than the symmetrical repetition of units within the symmetrical fields. Zuni rythm may be the very simplest of all rythms, the periodic repetition of a single motive, but somewhat more complex rhythms are sometimes used. Zuni artists are very fond of an alternating rythm, which seems to be required for the necks of jars. The usual Zuni arrangement of deer or spirals with sunflowers or panels is in reality a three part rythm when viewed horizontally, as all Zuni designs must be viewed. The three fundamental Zuni rythms are, therefore, a, a, a. . . .; a, b, a, b. . . .; a, b, b, a, b, b. . . . No examples were found of rhythmical groups of more than two distinct units. It is a firm conviction of all Zuni artists that this rhythmical repetition is very necessary. There was not one who did not scout the idea of painting a jar with one panel, and deer the rest of the way around, or with two panels on opposite sides of the jar, with two deer in one of the intervening sections, and three deer in the other.

In a style as narrowly circumscribed as that of Zuni, it is difficult to track down any general ideas on the harmoniousness of designs. In addition to the fixed rules for the use of each pattern, I heard a number of times one more general observation, namely, that it is not good to use the cloud-steps designs on the same jar with the deer and sunflower designs. This applies even to the bowls, where, as we have observed before, the greatest freedom is exercised in the combination of different patterns. In spite of the fact that all artists agree that there is no connection whatever between the designs used for the neck and the body of any jar, a study of a large number of jars reveals that there is a very definite relation. Practically all jars with the deer-sunflower pattern, or any of its variants, on the body, have the triangle-diamond combination on the neck (Nos. 76, 77), while almost all the jars with the simpler steps designs have on the neck the combination of the spiral and feather designs, (No. 79, A, B). All the patterns of this second group are simpler and more purely geometric in style than that of the first group, and the fact that they are always used together indicates a very definite feeling for general harmony of style. It is certainly felt that a No. 1 neck would not be appropriate on a No. 2 body, and the fact that this is never expressed does not make the feeling any less real.

Acoma

The form of the water jar at Acoma is about the same as that at Zuni, and, on the whole, is a very much more uniform product. In the decoration, however, we can immediately recognize two very distinctive styles, — a purely representative and a purely geometric type. The two types are kept strictly apart. Not only is the decorative content different, but also the whole approach to the decorative problem is utterly different, and the designs are developed according to entirely different principles. All women make both types and do not express preference for one type over the other. A detailed study of the output of different potters might reveal a different state of things; but this, of course, is not possible under present conditions. We must, therefore, believe the potter when she says, "I carry all the designs in my head and never get them mixed up." Certainly the two styles never mix,[8] — birds do not stray into the geometric patterns, and geometric motives and types of arrangement are not found on jars that favor the representative style.

The naturalistic is very much the simpler of the two types, and furthermore shows very much less variability. The forms presented

[8] There is a tendency at the present time, shown in the work of one potter, to use birds in otherwise geometric compositions. This is one symptom of the general disintegration of the older styles which is now beginning. See below, p. 38.

PLATE X

MODERN ACOMA JARS, AMNH

[30]

a

b

c

d

e

f

PLATE XI

Modern Acoma jars, AMNH

[31]

are always birds and plant forms. The bird is always represented under the same guise. It is always presented in profile, with curved beak, three or four separate tail feathers with rounded ends, a single pointed wing rising from the back. The heart is indicated, connected by a line with the mouth. Frequently it is nibbling at a branch of berries held in the claws. This creature has been variously identified by informants as parrot, turkey, chicken, but more frequently is designated merely as "bird." I prefer the term "bird." There does not seem to me to be any idea of representing any particular species and to identify it with any one is quite unnecessary. This bird design forms the basis of every jar containing decorations in this style. Generally two such birds appear on a jar, each framed in an arch of red or yellowish paint. Occasionally a rectangular ornament is used on each side between the two arches. Sprays of leaves and flowers fill the spaces within and without the arches. The favorite floral ornament is a round four-petalled flower, resembling a wild rose. The leaves are long and slender. Spikes of berries arranged in single or double rows along a stem are commonly used. The coloring is predominantly red on white. Black is used for stems, leaves, berries and for the outlines of all designs; but the birds, flowers and decorative arches are all executed in red or yellow. The whole patterning is very light, and the background is prominent. Jars of this type are shown on Pl. X.

None of the jars bearing bird and flower patterns vary very much from this type. Sometimes three, rather than two, of these birds are used. Rarely the arches are omitted, in which cases three or four birds are used, but on the whole, the type shows little variability.

At Sia a type of pottery is made which closely resembles the representative type of Acoma. Sia pottery is very often decorated with plant and animal forms, especially birds. The particular combination and arrangement which is found at Acoma occurs over and over at Sia. In fact, so similar are they that often it would be impossible to tell from the decoration alone whether the pot came from Acoma or Sia. However, the clay of Acoma is extraordinarily light, and fine, while that of Sia is coarse and heavy — heavier than that of Zuni — and dark in color. Considering the uniformity of this type at Acoma, in striking contrast with other types of design there, it would seem not unlikely that this type was introduced in fairly recent times from Sia, where it is the dominant style, and that it has been copied with little variation since that time.

Very much more interesting from every point of view is the geometric style of Acoma, which shows an exuberance of design unsurpassed anywhere in the Southwest, not excepting even the Hopi ware.

After the almost classic simplicity and clarity of Zuni design, the intricacy of Acoma ware seems to belong to another age or another civilization. All the structural forms which characterize Zuni ornament are absent in Acoma. Instead of the Zuni clarity of composition, its neat boxed-off appearance, its emphasis on structural lines and the recognition of the decorative value of white spaces, we have an almost Gothic exuberance of ornament, filling without break the whole surface of the jar from rim to base. The differentiation of neck from body, which is the first commandment of Zuni design is not generally recognized, and the background is completely covered in a manner to inspire horror in the heart of any Zuni artist. Structural lines are so broken and overlaid with ornament as to be wholly obscured. Moreover, there is a bewildering variety of design, that seems to defy all classification. At Zuni family resemblances between pots are strong, and identity is not uncommon. On the other hand, I cannot recall ever seeing two Acoma jars that are alike, and resemblances are not very close. All this wealth of design is constructed out of a very few elements, — fewer even than at Zuni. A considerable number are common to the two wares.

No help in solving the structural problems of Acoma design was to be had from the artists. Whereas a Zuni or Hopi woman can tell

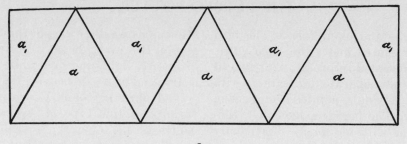

a

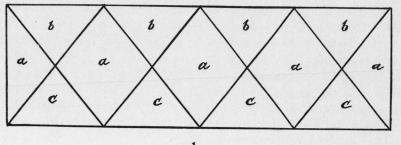

b

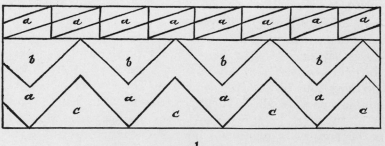

c

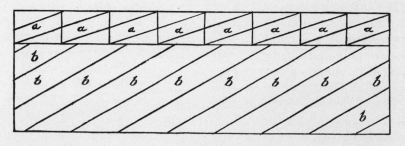

d

PLATE XII

DESIGN ARRANGEMENTS ON ACOMA JARS, AMNH

a, Pl. XI, a; b, AMNH; c, Pl. XI, c; d, Pl. XI, d

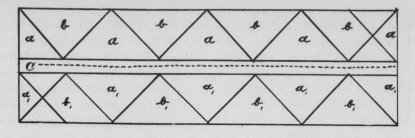

a

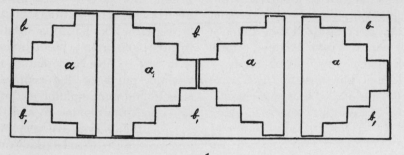

b

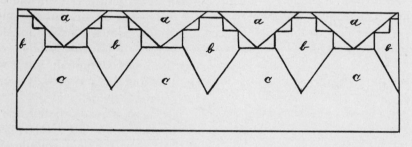

c

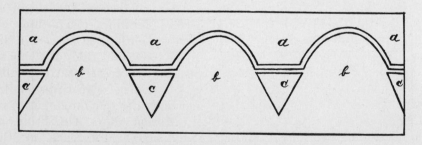

d

PLATE XIII

Design arrangements on Acoma jars, AMNH

a, AMNH; b, AMNH; c, Pl. XI, f; d, Pl. XI, e

you exactly how she builds her designs, I could not get this information from any Acoma informant. For the Acoma artist the unit of design is the jar. It is an indivisible whole; and no smaller units are recognized. To an Acoma painter the question of how many designs she uses and how she combines them is quite meaningless. From Zuni I was able to get a fairly complete set of the different design elements drawn by a native artist. I could not get anything like this from Acoma, because no one there recognized the existence of separate elements. From Laguna, whose art is strongly influenced by that of Acoma, I got design drawings, but most of these were drawings of pots, and not of design elements.

The following analysis is, therefore, based chiefly on a study of the large collection of 20th Century Acoma pottery in the American Museum of Natural History.

The form of the Acoma water jar is not very different from that of Zuni. The height is, perhaps, somewhat greater in proportion to circumference, and the neck a little longer. We have noted that Acoma jars do not show any break in outline between neck and body. However, these differences in proportion and outline are very slight. The decorative field, therefore, is of practically the same shape as at Zuni, an essentially horizontal field, divided into upper and lower sections by the swelling of the vessel. It is of fundamental importance that at Acoma the structural lines of the design do not follow the structural lines of the vessel. The horizontal lines of the vessel, which have their roots in the technique of horizontal coiling, are overlaid with designs whose prevailing lines are diagonal. Horizontal bands are occasionally used in Acoma decoration, but they are generally subordinated to a diagonal composition. Pl. XIII, a, is an example of a horizontal band interrupting what is essentially a diagonal design. The introduction of a diagonal composition opens up opportunity for endless variation which would be impossible in designs built out of vertical and horizontal lines alone. Plates XII, XIII show some of the simpler forms, all sketched from pots in the American Museum

of Natural History. Some of the jars from which these schematic drawings are made are shown in Plate XI. The great variety of design is, perhaps, due to the tendency of the artist to play with the structural lines of the designs. In dealing with a type of ornament where new combinations can be easily evolved by rearranging simple lines, the stimulus to the constant invention of new forms is very great. The method which prevails at Acoma of drawing the outlines of the designs in charcoal before painting would be favorable to this particular type of invention.

It will be observed that in most cases the various parts of the composition are not clearly and unmistakably set off from one another by lines or spaces, and the lines of the designs themselves are very much broken up and overlaid with subsidiary ornament. In Pl. XIII, b, a stepped figure is substituted for a diagonal line, while in Pl. XIII, a, b, the fundamental structure is even more obscured by the introduction of intersecting vertical or horizontal bands. Pl. XIII, d, shows a jar encircled by a curving ribbon of red, which hardly looks diagonal, until we notice the small triangular patterns, c, c, c, which fill out the diagonal fields.

We have already noted the tendency of Acoma designs to fill without break the whole of the decorative field, completely eliminating the background. This is the result of the way in which the Acoma painter approaches the problem of design. Instead of starting with certain familiar ornamental elements and constructing out of these a design that conforms to certain rules of composition, she reverses the process. Starting with the unbroken field as her decorative unit, she divides and redivides this into areas to receive paints of different colors. This brings us to another fundamental difference in the character of design at Acoma and Zuni. Whereas Zuni patterns are largely a handling of line, Acoma patterns are primarily a treatment of surfaces. "We have three kinds of designs," said one Acoma informant, "the red, the black and the striped designs." Naturally there is a plentiful use of paint in all these patterns.

We do not find large unbroken surfaces of one solid color, but the whole surface is covered over with paint of one color or another. The decoration is in four colors, the fine line hatchure constituting a fourth color. Wherever white occurs, it is part of the design. Frequently the white portions can be considered as the design for which the painted area serves as a background (Pl. XI, f). Negative painting[9] is characteristic of many places. The typical ware of Santo Domingo, for instance, is always decorated in this style, the principal elements being simple white forms arranged in bands upon a black background. Negative painting in this sense is never found at Acoma. Many patterns can be interpreted as white forms against a painted background, or as painted forms against a white background; the same design may be interpreted in both ways by two different observers. I am inclined to think that neither interpretation is correct, but rather that there is no background whatever, and that an equal decorative value has been assigned to each of the four colors used. The colors are combined so skillfully and so carefully balanced that in spite of the amount of surface covered, the designs always remain light and graceful.

Design is so overwhelmingly a matter of arrangement and color, that it seems profitless to attempt an analysis or classification of the decorative motives which are used, other than to note a few of the more important forms. Triangles are the most important single element, and are treated in a great variety of ways. The diagonal arrangement always produces triangles which, subdivided, produce more triangles. These are frequently painted in solid colors, sometimes with a white square left in the center. Triangular figures with slightly curved sides give rise to a graceful leaf pattern which is of frequent occurrence. One, three, or five slender leaf patterns in white are enclosed in a black triangle.

Squares and diamonds of solid colors are frequently used. They are often subdivided

diagonally into two or four triangles, generally painted in contrasting colors. A diamond divided into a checkerboard of nine small diamonds is a common motif.

Some of the simpler of the step designs which we have seen in Zuni are used. The steps are generally used in the form of a stepped band or ribbon.

Bands are ordinarily very simple in design. A checkerboard band, generally white with hatchure, is common. Even more common is a band composed of small triangles on alternate sides of a central line. The leaf design referred to above is sometimes arranged in bands. Diamonds with points touching are often used as a border.

The complete absence of spiral or circular forms should be noted.

The same motives which are used on full sized water jars are transferred to the diminutive pots made for the tourist trade. The patterns are not reduced in size to conform to the size of the vessel, but fewer units are used. Thus, where a large jar may contain thirty-six separate ornamental units, a little pot of similar shape, about four inches high, will contain but eight. In spite of this difference in the number of units used, the whole decorative scheme of the two pieces may be exactly alike, the difference being merely that the larger surfaces of the water jar require, in the artist's eye, a breaking up of the main divisions of the pattern into smaller and smaller units. This multiplication goes on within the large lines of the design, which do not vary very much for vessels of different size.

This whole style is exceedingly unstable. Pottery collected at Acoma fifty years ago and now in the United States National Museum shows decoration applied according to entirely different principles. (See Plate XIV.) The all-over tendency which is so marked a feature of present Acoma design was not apparent at that time Instead of many finely drawn designs covering the whole surface from base to rim, the decoration was laid on in bold patterns around the center of the jar, generally with a considerable amount

---

[9] Negative painting as a special technique is not used; the same effect is secured by ordnary techniques.

PLATE XIV

Old Acoma jars, about 1875, USNM

of undecorated background showing above and below. Four designs were generally used, interlocking and forming an irregular band. Sometimes the surface was fairly well covered, but there is never the slightest doubt that the patterns are painted on a background. The designs are very striking, and are executed with a liberal use of paint, so that in spite of the prominence of the background, the jars are generally darker in general effect than the present product. Birds are occasionally used. The emphasis on diagonal lines which underlies the present style of composition is completely lacking, although the germs of it may be seen in the free use of diamond shaped and oval patterns. The style is decidedly curvilinear.

Not only is the present style of recent origin, but also it is already showing signs of decay. Two foreign influences tend to change the style, first the commercial manufacture of little atrocities like baskets, cups, candlesticks, vases and the like, to which the highly developed and subtle style of ornament is not applicable; secondly, the revival of certain archaeological types, principally bowls with incurving rims, and the long-necked vases, decorated with interlocking key, or rarely, scroll figures, in black and hatchure. However, there seems to be something inherent in the style which is causing its decline, because even the most painstaking and skillful painters no longer adhere to the strict principles of composition. I have already mentioned the intrusion of representative forms into the geometric style. Furthermore, the patterns are all painted with greater freedom, the different parts run into one another and interlock, so that it is impossible to say where one division ends and the next begins. This growing formlessness is very much less pleasing than the highly formal style that preceded it. The rapid disintegration seems, however, to be characteristic of all all-over styles. When there is no longer any background to fill, the designs continue to spread, running into one another, regardless of structural lines, and the design becomes a background for something else. Boas has pointed out how this has

occurred under similar conditions in the case of the Chilkat blanket.[10] It appears to me that the same thing may have occurred in the case of Nasca pottery, where the form of composition is lost with the increasing elaboration of the pattern. However, the actual history of patterns and styles has not yet been traced in a sufficient number of cases to warrant the conclusion that this is a general development.

Hopi

The present style of Hopi pottery is a revival of the ancient type exemplified by the Sikyatki ware. This differs markedly in form, design and color from any modern ware, including that which was made in the Hopi villages until very recently. We have already noted the difference in the forms of vessels, we have now to see how this difference has affected the type of decoration. The shallow, wide-spreading water jar with the flat top and small mouth presents a decorative field of a shape entirely different from any we have so far encountered. The decoration is mainly on the flat top, but extends to a point somewhat below the shoulder. (See Pl. XV.) This field, viewed from above, presents the form of a broad ring with the small opening for the mouth in the center. The decoration is best considered in this way, and as a matter of fact is universally so considered by the Hopi potters. Not only does this change in the form of the field influence the form of the designs which fill it, but also by bringing the whole of the decorative field into the field of vision at the same time, exerts a subtle influence on the character of the designs and the integration of the whole composition.

The field is bordered at its inner edge with a broad black band, about three-eighths of an inch wide, which corresponds to the Zuni life line, and, like it, is always broken. A similar band, usually, but not always, unbroken, borders the outer edge.

Within this field the following arrangements are all common:

1. A continuous band, consisting of a single, fairly simple design, the most common design of this

10 Emmons: The Chilkat Blanket.

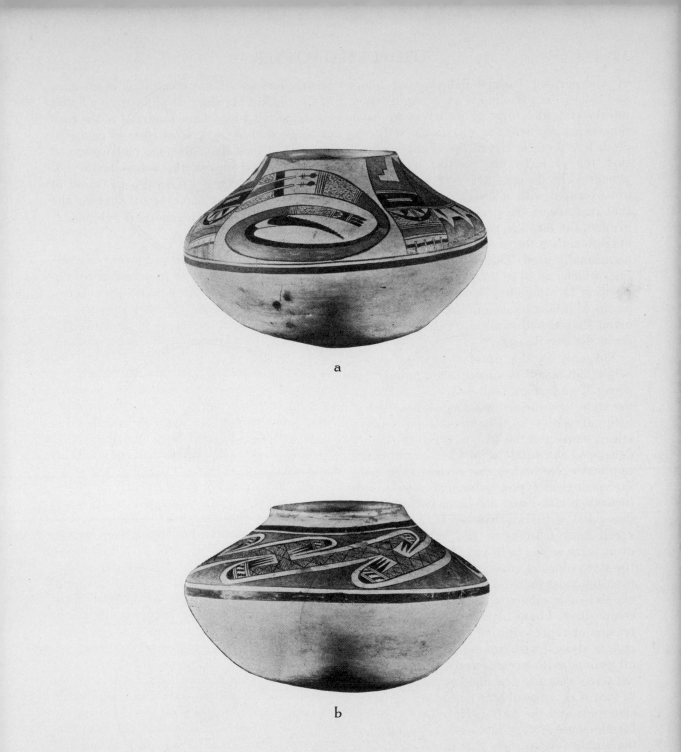

a

b

PLATE XV

MODERN HOPI JARS, AMNH

[39]

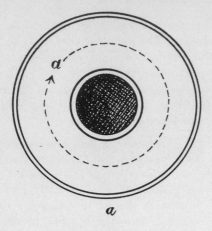

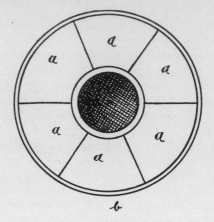

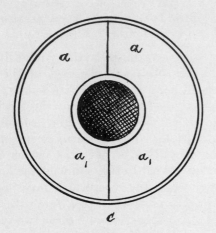

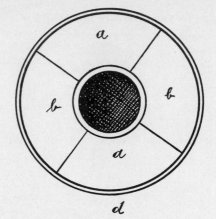

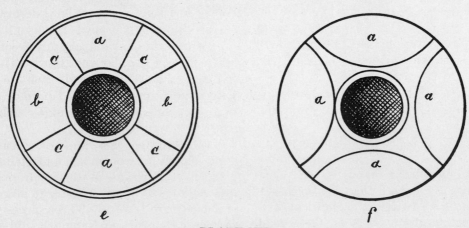

PLATE XVI

DESIGN ARRANGEMENTS ON HOPI JARS

type being a variant of a continuous scroll. (Pl. XV, b; XVI, a.

2. Division of the field into four, less frequently six, equal sections, containing the same pattern. (Pl. XVI, b.)

3. Division into two parts, each half containing a design which is completely symmetrical with regard to a central line. (Pl. XVI, c.)

4. Four divisions with alternating units. These divisions may or may not be of equal size. They are frequently paired in regard to size as well as pattern. (Pl. XV, a; XVI, d.)

5. Division into eight unequal units containing three designs. An elaboration of No. 4. (Pl. XVI, e.)

6. Where the outer bordering line is absent and the pattern is posed directly on the surface of the bowl, four similar designs are ordinarily used. Two types have been noted. (Pl. XVI, f.)

The most popular styles are 1, 2, and 4. Four designs are universally preferred.

It will be noted that all of these arrangements are comparatively simple. The more intricate of the Sikyatki designs, such as that which appears on Fewkes' famous "butterfly bowl" [11] are avoided. All the designs which I have noted are radiating designs, and I have seen no examples of a division of the field into inner and outer rings.

To quote Nampeyo, the founder and leading spirit of the Hopi school of decoration: "The best arrangement for the water jar is four designs around the top,—two and two, like this (indicating on the floor the arrangement). The designs opposite each other should be alike." Her own work clearly showed her preference for this type of arrangement.

Contrary to conditions elsewhere, the water jar is comparatively unimportant in Hopi ceramics. The characteristic Hopi vessel is the small bowl. This object ranges in size from four to ten inches in diameter, the greatest number being about seven inches across. Anything larger than ten inches is rarely made, the great mixing bowl of Zuni being completely absent. It is on these small bowls that the most typical Hopi patterns are found.

[11] Fewkes, 1899. Pl. CXXXV, b.

The general scheme of decoration is a single design. The greatest variety is to be found in the amount of field which is covered and the particular portion of the field which is chosen for decoration. Some of the more important types are shown in Plate XVII. These may be classified as follows:

1. The "one-line" design,—a crescent or horse shoe shaped design which follows closely the "road-line" just below the rim of the bowl, leaving the center of the bowl blank. (Pl. XVII, a.)

2. A crescent shaped or triangular motif, suspended from a darkened sector of the circular field. (Pl. XVII, b.)

3. A single design placed somewhat above the center of the bowl, with the largest massing of color in its upper portion. (Pl. XVII, c.)

In all these designs the "road-line" remains constant, and the rest of the design seems to hang from it. There seems to be no recognition of the center of the bowl. Even more or less detached designs are not placed in the center. The patterns seem all to be fundamentally rim patterns, which may or may not extend to the center of the bowl.

In contrast to these, which form the great mass of Hopi bowls, are a few with strictly radiating designs. Among these two types are predominant. (Pl. XVII, d.) These patterns are all strictly geometrical in marked contrast to the prevailingly representative patterns which constitute the mass bowl decorations.

The outer rims of bowls are usually decorated with a simple band, or more frequently a single simple, angular unit. Bowls with sharply incurved rims are decorated on the outside only with a simple panelled border, consisting of a single rectangular unit regularly repeated.

Large storage jars are still occasionally made. Not many women will undertake a work of such proportions. With the present careless methods of firing, disaster to large pieces is almost sure to result. Three pieces which I saw were the work of Nampeyo, and all were decorated with very similar designs. Two large designs covered the whole surface. The square field was divided into four quarters, and a narrow vertical panel. The sun was symbolically represented on the panel, and in the four rectangles were represented various features of the earth and sky. The design in its elements and arrangement was different from every other Hopi design, and very much cruder.

Canteens designed for household use are made of red clay undecorated. Diminutive sizes are made for sale, and these are decorated with designs of the type used on bowls. The circular field of the canteen is treated in much the same way.

Vases of several forms are made in imitation of imported articles. The most popular type is a high narrow vase with flat top and no neck, tapering gradually from shoulder to base. These are decorated with a broad band around the upper portion. The band is generally composed of alternating rectangular or diagonal units. Occasionally typical bowl designs are elongated and fitted to the vase form. One or two such patterns may be used.

With the exception of the last two purely commercial items, the vase and the decorated canteen, we find among the Hopi the same highly developed sense of the appropriateness of designs which we have already observed among the Zuni. The design that is considered suitable for the bowl is not used on the water jar, and vice versa. The decoration of the water jar is very much more formal than that of the bowl. The confining of the design within parallel lines, and the division of the field so formed into clearly differentiated units all contribute to the formality of the design. The character of the decorative motifs is correspondingly less free on the water jar than on bowls. Water-jar patterns are very largely geometric and angular. If they had representative ancestors, they are so far removed that considerable speculation is required to determine what they were. We have already commented on the striking frequency of duplicating symmetry in these designs. This is a trait sufficiently rare in pueblo art to be deserving of very particular emphasis.

The bowl designs used by the Hopi show the highest development of conventionalized representation, in which bird forms predominate. There are a large number of fairly realistic birds, some that are barely recognizable, and many patterns which considered singly have no bird-like characteristics. But these, nevertheless, make use of the same parts which characterize the more realistic birds, and must, therefore, also be considered as bird derivatives. These designs have all been suggested by the designs on ancient Sikyatki pottery, fully described in Fewkes' admirably illustrated volumes.[12] Hopi designs sketched by native artists are shown in Plates XXXIII and XXXIV, Appendix II.

Much of the charm of Hopi pottery is due to its attractive coloring. The Hopi potters do not use a white slip, but make their pots of a clay which fires to various shades of cream and yellow. Owing to the nature of the clay, or the methods of firing, or to both, the clay never fires evenly, and the same vessel shows all tones from palest ivory to a deep cream flushed softly with rose. Against this pleasing background the designs are laid in brown and red paint. Although this soft blending of colors adds greatly to the attractiveness of the ware, it is obvious that the Hopis are not colorists in the sense that the Acoma potters are. Hopi designs would lose none of their fundamental significance if executed in black and white. Like the Zuni designs they depend for their effectiveness on the subtle manipulation of line alone. The Hopi potters are the pre-eminent masters of line, and like all masters, are well aware of the importance of simplicity. "For the bowl I always use a one-line design. It must start from the 'road line,' and come back into it again." (Nampeyo.) All potters when describing the way in which they copy the patterns from scraps of ancient pottery spoke of studying the fragments "to get the line of the design."

San Ildefonso

In turning to the contemporary ceramic art of San Ildefonso, we are confronted by a decorative problem quite different from any thus

12 Fewkes, R B A E 17, 33.

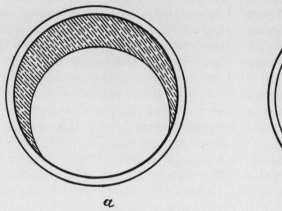

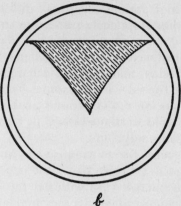

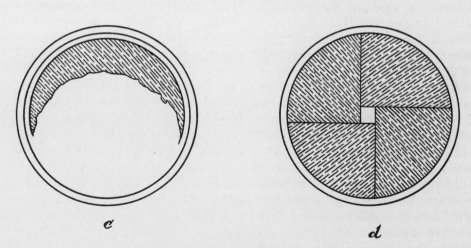

PLATE XVII

Design arrangements on Hopi bowls

far considered. We have heretofore described only painted wares, all similar in that the decorative effect is achieved by contrast in color, the pattern being applied in dark pigments against a white or light colored background. At San Ildefonso painted wares of this kind have recently been superseded by something different, — an all black ware which depends for decorative effect upon the manipulation of surface finish alone. Polished black ware has been made at one time or another at all the eastern pueblos. It has always been made in small quantities at San Ildefonso along with the more common painted wares; and at the neighboring village of Santa Clara it has in modern times been the characteristic ceramic product. The process by which the distinctive decorated ware of San Ildefonso is made has already been described (p. 11 f.). In that place we pointed out the care that is lavished on the molding and polishing. The beauty of these vessels lies in the perfection of finish; ornament is intended merely to bring out by contrast the beauty of the deep lustrous polish. Native potters are well aware of this.

The forms of the vessels are varied, and many represent types recently introduced by white purchasers. These include bowls of various shapes, tall vases designed to serve as lamp bases, and even cigarette boxes and ash trays. The vessels are all small in size and exquisitely molded. The most popular form is still the shallow bowl with incurved rim, such as has been made at one time or another in every pueblo. Deep globular or melon shaped bowls are also made in large numbers. These are all small, rarely exceeding eight inches in diameter. One woman occasionally makes large water jars similar in form to those of Santa Clara.

On all the bowls the sole decoration is the narrow band, sometimes only a row of tiny scallops, around the rim. This band is rarely more than two inches wide. The width and placing of the border depend in some measure upon the size and shape of the vessel. Olla bowls with slightly flattened rims and a marked angle at the shoulder are decorated on the rims only, i.e. above the angle of the shoulder. Deep bowls with unbroken curve from rim to base are usually decorated around the rim, rarely with a broad band (two to two and one-half inches) around the portion of greatest diameter. Shallow bowls are always decorated on the outer rims only, the decoration frequently extending well below the curve of the shoulder. Beyond these few inevitable distinctions, the width and character of the border seem in no way dependent upon the size or shape of the vessel. The choice seems largely a matter of individual preference. I have seen, for instance, the same border of tiny scallops used as the sole ornament on a small shallow dish, and on one of the largest and handsomest of the melon shaped bowls that I found in the pueblo. Both were the work of the same man, to whom we shall have occasion to refer many times.

The bands employed show considerable variety, based on a very small number of motives. Both continuous and panelled bands are used, panelling being preferred for all wider bands.

On some vessels, especially on small-mouthed and rather flat-topped olla bowls, alternating panels, containing different units are used; sometimes three different units are arranged so that similar units occupy opposite sides of the vessel (a b a c a b a c). The alternation of two different units is not uncommon in shallow bowls also. However, the most frequent arrangement is the repetition of a single unit. Even here, there is a marked preference for even numbers, especially four. More than half the panelled borders analyzed are divided into four units, a scheme which is probably dictated by technical considerations. As at Zuni, the whole field is blocked off into rectangular spaces before the painting of the actual designs is begun, frequently before the design is chosen. In laying out this framework, it is easier to achieve accurate spacing by a division into four quarters than by any other division. Division into five parts has been observed once, six several times, and eight is not uncommon.

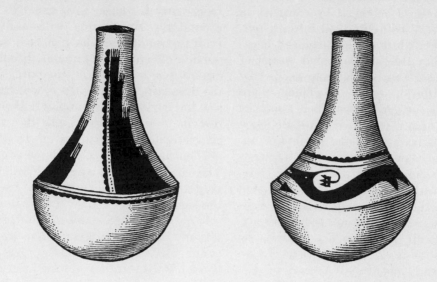

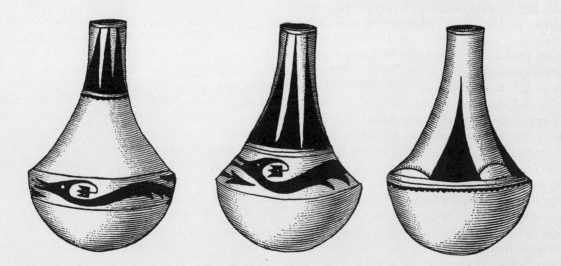

PLATE XVIII

MODERN VASES FROM SAN ILDEFONSO

[45]

San Ildefonso designs are shown in Appendix III. The design which appears more frequently than any other, is the *avanyu* or horned serpent (No. 1). It is always represented in the same form, which has undoubtedly been derived from some ceremonial object. It did not exist in the present form as a pottery design even on meal bowls prior to the recent ceramic revival, and seems to have no close relation with the other strictly geometrical patterns that are now used.

Among the continuous bands, arrangements of scallops, triangles and frets are prominent. The elements are few in number, and the combinations for the most part are simple, although by no means lacking in variety. The panelled bands show greater inventiveness, but these too are based on a very small number of ornamental motives. In their handling there is a decided preference for diagonal compositions. The diagonal division is always from the lower left to upper right hand corners of the rectangular field, and the two triangular spaces thus formed are occupied by distinct but carefully balanced motives. The most conspicuous of these elements is a fan shaped motive, which is probably a conventionalized bird or feather. This appears in many variants in combination with frets and terraced figures. (See Nos. 13, 17, 18, 19, 23, 24, 28, 29.) Another important and distinctive motive is usually designated as the "leaf" design (Nos. 22, 23, 25, 27.) Other patterns are for the most part combinations of frets and terraced figures.

More interesting than the decoration of bowls is the treatment of unfamiliar forms such as high vases, tobacco boxes and plates. Of these the most striking are the high vases. Pl. XVIII shows five, all the work of one potter. There seems to be no fixity in regard to decorative zones, or the types of ornament used. There may be a single band around the widest portion of the vessel (No. 2); two bands, one around the widest part and one around the upper rim (No. 3); or the decoration may all be on the neck and shoulder (Nos. 1, 4, 5). The types of ornament used show great variety, many of the motives ordinarily used on bowls being adapted to these unfamiliar forms. For rectangular boxes, panelled designs similar to those used on bowls are employed. I did not happen to see any actual duplication of bowl designs on boxes, but the general treatment of the rectangular field, the prevalence of diagonal composition, and the motives employed are all so similar that it is likely that the same designs have been transferred from one form to the other. (See Nos. 35-38 for box designs.)

The same might also be said in regard to the decoration of flat plates. For these radiating designs are always used, — the field being divided into quadrants. Two which are very typical are shown in Nos. 39, 40. These show exactly the same motives adapted to the circular field. The flat plate is not a common form; it has only recently been introduced and its decoration is not yet highly developed.

The outstanding characteristic of San Ildefonso design is its restraint and brevity of expression. The restriction of decoration to comparatively narrow bands, the use of panelling in all but the narrowest and simplest borders, the small number of ornamental elements employed, combine to produce a formalism which, however, is never stereotyped. In addition to the formality of the arrangement, the exigencies of the particular technique tend to produce a restrained and chastened form of decoration. Striking effects in patterning can never be achieved with dull and polished black surfaces. The dull paint serves only to intensify and throw into relief the brilliant surface of the vessel, which constitutes its greatest charm. For this purpose a sparing use of dull surface, with a careful balancing of masses is most effective. Line is unimportant, and elaboration of detail destroys rather than enhances the effect. This fact is clearly recognized by the potters themselves, who are unanimous in saying that the most important thing to be considered is the surface finish. Ornament is always considered incidental. The potters expend infinite pains in the laborious and time-consuming process of polishing, going over the surface again and

a

b

c

d

e

PLATE XIX

f

SAN ILDEFONSO PAINTED JARS, END OF NINETEENTH CENTURY, AMNH

[47]

again, even after it appears to the uninitiated to be perfect. The painting takes relatively little time, and seems not to receive the same scrupulous and painstaking attention as the polishing. Technically the decoration is excellent; the spacing is accurate, the lines are true, the surface paint evenly applied. Furthermore, there is no sterile repetition of the same patterns. In a collection of twenty-five bowls, all made by one family in the course of a few days, I found seventeen different border designs. The only pattern that appeared more than once in this collection was the *avanyu*, already referred to, which was represented eight times, with only slight variations. This variability of design within the limits of the style are characteristic also of the work of all other potters whose work I observed. A comparison of the contemporary style with the rather flamboyant decoration that immediately preceded it and which is frequently the work of the same artists, shows how far reaching have been the effects of the change in technique upon decorative style. (See Pl. XIX.)

In addition to the black ware just described, a similar ware in red is made in small quantities. The two wares are identical. It is only in the firing that any distinction is made. A woman making a large batch of pottery will decide when all are decorated which to leave red and which to fire to black. Those that are to remain red are removed from the fire before it is smothered by the addition of fine fuel. There is, therefore, no need to consider this ware separately from the black already described.

Occasionally there are made in the pueblo a few pieces of the old polychrome or black on red pottery. I did not see a single piece of either type in work during my visit in 1925, although all women said they knew how to make both. However, a few pieces were offered for sale, and a few more were found in the shops of Santa Fé. These were all very poorly made and decorated. The surface was dull and chalky, the black pigment a dull slaty gray. The decorations were all in the florid style that preceded the dominance of polished wares. It is very possible that these pieces are the remnants of a ware now completely obsolete, which their owners have never been able to sell because of their inferior workmanship. At any rate, the material is too meagre to make any analysis profitable.

IV

THE PERSONAL ELEMENT IN DESIGN

We are now ready to return to our potter, whom we left some time back, holding in her hands the carefully molded and polished vessel, ready to receive its painted decoration. What will she do with this gleaming white or yellow or black surface? What is in her mind as she turns the vessel over in her hands, studying its proportions with reference to the style of decoration traditional in her group? Up to this point she has been guided wholly by sense and intuition. Her appreciation of form and surface is non-intellectual and non-analytical. But the manipulation of design involves something more. "Anyone can make a good shape, but you have to use your head in putting on the design," as the pueblo potter naively remarks. This same comment has been heard from many women in many different villages and is their recognition of mental processes of different orders. The relative importance of rational and non-rational functions in the creation of these artistic products will become clearer in the following pages. Whether the potter actually constructs her designs intelligently, or merely rationalizes about them, the tendency to analyze is always present. She can always give an *ex post facto* explanation of design, but never of form.

The Planning of Designs

The frame of mind in which the artists approach the problem of decorating a pot may best be described in their own words:

While I am making a jar, I think all the time I am working with the clay about what kind of a design I am going to paint on it. When I am ready,

I just sit and think what I shall paint. I do not look at anything but just think what I shall draw and then when the pot is dry, I draw it. . . . I think about designs all the time. . . . I always know just how it will look before I start to paint. (Zuni.)

I always know the whole design before I start to paint. (Zuni.)

When I have finished with the shape, my thoughts are always on the design that I shall put on. Generally I have the whole design in my head before I begin to paint. (Laguna.)

All the time when I am not working, I am thinking about what designs I shall make, and when I start to paint, I have it all in my mind. (Hopi.)

I think about designs when I am working and I have the whole design in my head before I start to paint. (Hopi.)

Whenever I am ready to paint, I just close my eyes and see the design, and then I paint it. (Hopi.)

I could continue to quote statements of this kind. However, I think this is sufficient to show that the whole scheme of decoration is most carefully planned and is fixed in the mind of the artist before she begins on any part of her design. Only one informant did not "see just how it will look" before starting to paint, although several admitted that their achievements often fell short of their original plan. Of course we must not take too literally the statements of the artists that they never deviate from the chosen plan. We need only examine pottery to see numerous examples of asymmetries, cases where the original plan is not fully carried out. This is particularly true in the case of fillers which are not always used consistently throughout the vessel, — sometimes because irregular spacing makes this impossible, but frequently for no apparent reason save the artist's carelessness in carrying out her plan. Sometimes designs of this character are differently painted on the same jar, red hatching being used in one place and black in another, although the intention was unmistakably to make them alike. Nevertheless, in spite of these accidental deviations, there can be no question that as a rule the pottery is painted in accordance with a carefully considered plan, which has been worked out in detail in the mind of the artist before the first stroke appears on the jar.

At San Ildefonso, where the chief concern of the potter is the technical excellence of her work, especially perfection of modelling and brilliance of polish, the actual painting seems to be done without any preconceived plan. The band to be decorated is blocked off into rectangles and the designs are then fitted in. A potter will frequently pause when the design is half finished and study out how she shall complete it, tracing with the tip of her finger various possibilities, and selecting the one which seems best to fit the particular space. This hesitation, however, is rare among pueblo potters. Most of them study for a long time the undecorated form, but, having once started to paint, they proceed without pause until the design is finished.

The care with which the general scheme of decoration is planned extends also to the adjustment of the design to the field and to the actual painting. Nothing could be further from the truth than the usual picture of the pueblo potter, sitting down and casually covering jars with free-hand designs, with only her instinct to guide her brush. The perfect spacing of decoration on pottery is not achieved in this hit or miss fashion. The potter is fully aware of the technical difficulties of her work, and the greatest care is taken to overcome them. All potters measure the surfaces of their jars in one way or another. They do not use tape-measures and dividers but with their ten fingers are able to take fairly accurate measurements.

Before I start to paint, I measure with my thumb and finger all around the jar. First I measure for the large designs. If it doesn't come out right, I measure again, putting a small design between the large ones. I know just how it will look before I start. Then I measure with my fingers flat against the jar for the spaces between the different parts and for the thickness of the designs. If I start to paint before it is all measured, then I get nervous that it may not come out right. (Zuni.)

I should teach a girl to measure the jar with her hands so that the designs will come out even. First she should measure around the top. For a small jar the designs should be about two fingers apart, for a medium sized jar about a span. I mark the places where the designs will come with my nail. (Zuni.)

All women with whom I talked said that they measured their designs in this way. The most usual measurement is the distance between the thumb and the tip of the middle finger. There is a considerable individual variation in the amount of measuring that is done. Some women, such as the one first quoted above, measure their designs with great care. She is an old woman, — an expert potter who has been making pottery for about forty years and is thoroughly familiar with all designs. Her method of decorating a water jar was as follows:

First she studied carefully for some minutes the undecorated form, turning it around in her hands. Then she measured hastily with her thumb and middle finger the greatest circumference of the jar. Then she drew in the outlines of the first design, which was to be used four times around the jar. After the first element was completed, she measured it and the remaining space and drew in the second element. The two together occupied a little more than half the space, so the remaining two had to be slightly crowded, but this was hardly perceptible in the finished object. After drawing in outline the fillers and the design on the neck, she went over the whole jar, putting in the detail, such as hatchure, red fillings, etc.

This is the usual procedure among the potters of Zuni, Laguna and Isleta. At Acoma where a more intricate decorative scheme prevails even more care is used in the planning of the design. Here the usual method is to sketch the designs on the jar in charcoal, erasing whatever fails to please and correcting any errors in spacing.

First I draw in the design .with charcoal, and if it does not look right, I rub it out and draw it over again and if it is not right, I rub it out again and do it over. Sometimes I rub it out two or three times before it is right.

I have seen this method in use, and wherever I inquired, I found it to be the common practice of Acoma potters.

The Hopi women frequently draw their designs somewhere before painting them on pots. The more sophisticated women use pencil and paper, the others use the more primitive implements of finger nails on adobe floors. When I asked one woman whether she first drew her designs on paper, she was rather offended. "No. We draw them in our heads." But further questioning elicited the fact that she drew them on the floor first. "just to see how they will look."

The Sources of Design

The seriousness of these potters goes deeper than concern with the technical excellence of their products. We shall discuss elsewhere the religious associations which attach themselves to pottery designs. But aside from this, the importance which they attach to the purely esthetic aspects of pottery design is greater than is ordinarily assumed. Most of these women display the same symptoms which are common to creative artists among more sophisticated people. They all speak of sleepless nights spent in thinking of designs for the pot to be decorated in the morning, of dreams of new patterns which on waking they try and often fail to recapture, and above all, the constant preoccupation with decorative problems even while they are engaged in other kinds of work. The following quotations from a number of different women all illustrate this earnestness. That this is not a pose assumed before a foreigner and a prospective buyer is indicated in a remark made by an expert Zuni potter to me, — the potter being a very matter-of-fact person who was not blessed with the artistic temperament. She laughed heartily at the idea of dreaming about designs. "I never dream about designs. I know some women dream about them, but only the women who don't know how to paint dream about it. I always know just what I want to paint, and so I don't dream about it, and I don't worry about it."

Regarding the sources of design women speak as follows:

I am always thinking about designs, even when I am doing other things, and whenever I close my eyes, I see designs in front of me. I often dream of designs, and whenever I am ready to paint, I close my eyes and then the designs just come to me. I paint them as I see them. (Hopi.)

One night I dreamed and saw lots of large jars and they all had designs on them. I looked at them and got the designs in my head and next morning I painted them. I often dream about designs, and if I can remember them, I paint them. (Hopi.)

I think about designs all the time. Sometimes when I have to paint a pot, I can't think what design to put on it. Then I go to bed thinking about it all the time. Then when I go to sleep, I dream about designs. I can't always remember them in the morning, but if I do, then I paint that on the pot. (Zuni.)

While I am making a jar, I think all the time I am working with the clay about what kind of a design I am going to paint on it. When I am ready to paint, I just sit and think what I shall paint. (Zuni.)

I get all my ideas from my thoughts. I think of my thoughts as a person who tells me what to do. I dream about designs too. Sometimes before I go to bed, I am thinking about how I shall paint the next piece, and then I dream about it. I remember the designs well enough to paint in the morning. That is why my designs are better than those of other women. Some people do not think that pottery is anything, but it means a great deal to me. It is something sacred. I try to paint all my thoughts on my pottery. (Laguna.)

I never copy other women's designs. I use all the old Laguna designs. . . . I used to watch my aunt while she made pottery because she was such a good potter. That is how I learned to paint. (Laguna.)

I make up all my designs and never copy. I learned this design from my mother. I learned most of my designs from my mother. (Laguna.)

I never use other women's designs, and they never use mine. . . . I always have lots of designs in my head and never mix them. (Hopi.)

I like all kinds of designs. My jars are all different. I don't make the same design twice. Sometimes I make two or three alike, but not often. I don't like to do that. (Acoma.)

I like best to make new designs. I never copy other women's designs. Sometimes I see a design I like on a jar and if I want to make it, I ask the woman to give it to me. It would not be right to use another woman's design without asking. (Zuni.)

This is a new design. I learned the different parts of it from my mother, but they are put together in a new way. I always make new designs. I never copy the designs of other women. It is not right to do that. You must think out all your designs yourself. Only those who do not know copy. (Zuni.)

I go down to the ancient village and pick up pieces of pottery and try to put them together and get the line of the design. I never use other women's designs and they never use mine. . . . When I am not working, I think about what designs I will make and when I start to paint, I have it all in my mind. (Hopi.)

Nampeyo is my mother's sister, and she teaches me designs. When I find a piece of old pottery, I save it and get the design in my mind. Once I dreamed and saw lots of large jars and they had designs on them. I looked at them and got the designs in my mind and in the morning I remembered them and painted them. I often dream about designs and sometimes I remember them, and then I always use them. . . . I always use different designs. (Hopi.)

I save all the pieces of old pottery and try to work out the whole design from these scraps. Sometimes I use one of the old designs around the rim of a jar and make the rest of the design out of my head. I think about designs when I am not working and have the whole design in my head before I start to paint. Once I made a jar that I dreamed about. (Hopi.)

When I am ready to paint, I think how I am going to paint. I pick out pieces from the old village where I have my peach trees and try to get the line of the design and think how it went. I put the pieces together and pick out the best. That is how I learned to paint, from copying the old designs. When I first started to paint, I always used the designs from the old pottery, but now I sometimes make up new designs of my own. I always think about pottery even when I am doing other things. When I dream about designs, I paint them the next day. Whenever I close my eyes, I see the designs right in front of me. When I dream about designs, they are always new designs. When I am ready to paint, I just close my eyes and see the design and then I paint it. The designs just come to me, and I paint them as I see them. Every woman paints differently. (Hopi.)

It is apparent from these few extracts that not only does a great deal of thought go into the creation of these objects, but also there seems to be a definite attempt to make them a vehicle for personal experience. To say, "We paint our thoughts," is common in the villages where designs are clothed with symbolic meaning. But even where symbolism plays no role in decoration, as for instance, among the Acoma and the Hopi, there is nevertheless a strong feeling that each pot is an individual and a significant creation. The condemnation of copying the designs of other women is unanimous. All women denied copying from other potters, and most of them disclaimed repetition of their own designs. Even at Zuni where the inventive faculty is at a low ebb and where choice of design is narrowly circumscribed by prevailing taste, in spite of all this, each pot is approached as a new creation, the decoration of which is evolved only after much thought and inner communings. However much theory and practice may be at variance, there can be no doubt concerning the theory. And strangely enough, it is at Zuni where the ideal is stated with the deepest conviction that it is most frequently violated. This discrepancy between theory and practice in the invention of designs might be paralleled in our own and other civilizations.

The psychological implications of this very simple and rather amusing condition are profound and far-reaching, and rather disconcerting in the light they throw upon the workings of the human mind. There are other factors besides sterility of imagination involved. A woman in all sincerity reproduces a familiar type of ornament, believing it to be something derived from her own consciousness. The decorative content and treatment are long since familiar to the ethnologist; he can analyze the whole pattern into definite well known motives which regularly appear together, and the details of arrangement are those already noted for these motives. An analysis of the material with the potter is illuminating. She is puzzled and somewhat chagrined to have it pointed out that she has used three designs on the jar, although she has frequently expressed a decided preference for four designs. She can offer but one explanation: "We always use three when we make this design." They always *do* use three in this particular design, but of this fact, so striking to the ethnologist, she has never before thought. She is also much interested to have pointed out to her that the particular rim design chosen is invariably used with this body design and one other of similar character, but is never used in association with the very different deer and sunflower design. "Yes, that is right. We always do it that way, but I never thought about it before." As a matter of fact, however much she may rationalize, she has probably never thought about the design, its structure, or its elements, at all. She has experienced it unanalytically as a configuration, just as she has experienced the forms of her vessels. The design is a constellation of which the essential part is a relationship. The various elements may later be abstracted, as words may be isolated from the sentences of a naive speaker, who for many years has been correctly speaking his native tongue, though innocent of the simplest rules of grammar. In art, as in language, it is not difficult to bring into consciousness these unexpressed feelings for formal relationships.

One important point that is implicit, rather than explicitly expressed in the statements of the women, is the importance of the visual image in the creation of design. Only one woman speaks of shutting her eyes and seeing designs, but it seems safe to infer that all the women who speak of seeing "just how it will look" have a perceptual rather than an intellectual approach to the artistic problem. At Zuni, where principles of design are clearly recognized and where, furthermore, religious ideas are associated with designs, we might expect to find a strengthening of the intellectual point of view at the expense of the more purely esthetic, but so far as our information goes, this does not seem to be the case. Here as elsewhere, sensation and intuition play a larger role than intellect in the creation of design. The very inarticulateness of the artists on all general problems of expression favors a conclusion which cannot be documented.

This is quite consistent with the prevailingly unanalytical attitude towards design exhibited in native terminology. The whole question of symbolism will be dealt with in another place; we are here concerned only with the character of native design names. Confining our remarks to Zuni, where the evidence is fullest, and where the analytical tendency is most marked, we find that although it is possible to get a "name" for any design, anything in the nature of a fixed terminology is quite unknown. The woman from whom this information was obtained drew for me a series of what, to her, were the elements of Zuni design. These are by no means "elements" in any sense that would satisfy a scientist analyzing the decorative content of a style. They are rather patterns, — each consisting of a number of elements conveniently arranged for use on a certain part of a vessel. They are units in a psychological, but not in an objective sense. In connection with each of these compositions, I was able to get names of a sort. The name was sometimes applied to the whole pattern, sometimes only the elements were named, sometimes both the patterns and the elements received designations. There was no consistent principle apparent in the terminology. Furthermore, terms themselves are inconsistently applied. The same element is called in one composition "cloud," in another "flower," in yet another "drumstick." Furthermore, the same composition, with all its parts, will be differently named by the same person at different times. There is also a notable paucity of terms of a purely descriptive character, such as square, circle, triangle, and the like, although the language is not lacking in precise terminology of spatial concepts.

The total composition suggests a situation, generally of ceremonial or meteorological character, and the various elements are labelled in accordance with the situation thus suggested. The only design names which evoke an image are those of frankly representative designs such as the deer. Names such as "cloud" even when characterized as "red" or "black" or "striped," which are applied indiscriminately to designs showing no objective resemblance to clouds or to one another cannot possibly evoke an image. We must conclude that there is no design terminology at Zuni; in other villages the association of names and patterns is even more tenuous. Zuni design No. 5 has no name which would distinguish from innumerable other "cloud" designs, and yet it is correctly reproduced over and over again, and is always treated in precisely the same way. The lack of linguistic designation would indicate that it is always experienced as a sensual rather than an intellectual experience. It is fairly safe to assume that an experience to which a people has given no linguistic expression cannot be the object of rational thought, no matter how potent it may be on other planes of mental activity. Art, among pueblo Indians, as among ourselves, is something felt rather than discussed.

The great source of decorative ideas is, of course, tradition. This has frequently been reported about primitive art, and the present evidence strengthens this conclusion. All women state that they learned from their mothers not only the technique of pottery making, but also the particular designs and style of decoration which they use. Where they have learned designs from other sources as well, they generally express a preference for the "old designs," always meaning by this the designs used by their mothers. The reason for the preponderance of tradition is not far to seek. It lies largely in practical considerations. A woman who must make a pot to hold the family supply of water will ordinarily reproduce more or less accurately a familiar pattern. It is the simple and obvious solution to her problem, and has nothing whatever to do with artistic problems, except in so far as it may be an index of popular taste. Objects of traditional style may be of interest to the collector, but it is in the departures from tradition, whether great or slight, that we must study the workings of the artistic impulse. It is therefore of particular significance, not that all women mention their mothers' teachings, which is natural, but that practically all recognize other sources of inspiration as well.

Of these other sources the one most frequently mentioned, generally in response to direct inquiry, was dreams. As in many cases specific dreamed designs were shown to me, I have no doubt that the experiences were genuine. Of course, considered objectively, dreamed designs are no less traditional than designs learned from the potter's mother. Wherever dreamed designs were shown to me they were in the traditional, or more correctly, popular style of the village. When Hopi potters dream designs they are always in the accepted Sikyatki manner, just as twenty years ago they would have been in the style prevailing at that time. Nevertheless, from the standpoint of psychology of artistic creation, it is two entirely different things to dream a design and to copy one. The importance of dreamed designs in other areas, as, for instance, in Plains beadwork or Plateau basketry, has been frequently pointed out. I could not find that in the pueblos any special significance, religious or otherwise, was attached to dreamed designs, or that they were considered as more intimately personal than designs derived from other sources.

After dreams, and more important than them, the most frequently mentioned source of design is ancient pottery. This is a particularly rich source of inspiration on First Mesa, where all the contemporary pottery is made in imitation of the beautiful ware of Sikyatki. The ruin of Sikyatki is about two miles northeast of Hano and the women go there, especially after heavy rains, and gather potsherds from the great quantities that cover the mound. So far as I have been able to learn, they do not do any systematic digging for pottery below the surface. All the pieces shown to me were the smallest sherds, with the merest fragments of designs. Better pieces are sometimes found but they are immediately sold to traders, as good picees of Sikyatki ware command high prices. When a woman finds a piece of pottery with good painting, she tries to study out "the line of the design," her own imagination and her knowledge and feeling for the Sikyatki style filling in the gaps in the very fragmentary material.

It is very difficult to estimate to what extent this new pottery is merely an imitation of the Sikyatki and to what extent it is a veritable revival of the ancient style. In the first place, the so-called Sikyatki is by no means a uniform style. At least two distinct types are found in the Sikyatki ruin. In one the yellow ground is decorated with simple patterns in brownish-black. The patterns are almost exclusively geometrical and angular, and there is a preference for a division of the circular field [1] into quadrants, only one of which in many cases is decorated. When the four quadrants are decorated, opposite sides are paired. In most cases the designs are crudely drawn, but many excellently made pieces have been recovered.[2]

The other type of ware found at Sikyatki is a true polychrome with curvilinear designs in which life forms predominate. The patterns on the whole are more elaborate in conception and more skillfully executed. In some cases the technique of spattering is used in addition to the usual brushwork. In this ware alone all degrees of complexity of design and perfection of technique may be observed. I am confident that the large mass of material that goes under the name of Sikyatki can be separated into a number of distinct sub-types on the basis of decorative style. Whether or not these types are contemporaneous is another question, and one that cannot now be answered though it is of the greatest importance. It should also be borne in mind that the famous Sikyatki finds are all mortuary pottery and a study of household wares as represented in sherds may reveal still other types.

In the face of the wide range of Sikyatki designs, the modern Hopi women are discriminating connoisseurs. Although their work is often crude and always hasty, they select their designs invariably from the more elaborate and skillfully painted Sikyatki specimens. This makes the modern style very much more uniform and also more elaborate than a random selection from the graves of Sikyatki. There is one notable exception. One potter, an excellent craftsman, one of the very best, shows a marked preference for the earlier, simpler Sikyatki ware, and her bowls with angular designs executed with great delicacy and precision are among the most striking and beautiful of Hopi products. Fewkes reports that he found no two Sikyatki pieces exactly alike. The same might almost be said of modern Hopi ware. In a collection of several hundred pieces on the shelves of the trader's store, it would be difficult to find any duplicates, and although several variants of the same general form might be found, these variants will show considerable diversity. In a style as varied as this, in order to see how accurately the Hopi potter copies her Sikyatki model it would be necessary to compare

[1] In Sikyatki, as in modern Hopi, the bowl is the characteristic form.

[2] Dr. Kidder also has noted the sharp differentiation of Sikyatki ware, and has given the type just described, which he considers an earlier form, the name Jeddito.

each piece with its Sikyatki prototype, a procedure obviously impossible, even if the prototypes existed. However, a number of facts point to the conclusion that the copying of Sikyatki pieces is by no means as slavish as is claimed by ethnologists and by many of the women themselves.

In the first place, although I have watched many Hopi women decorating pottery, I have never seen one of them copying from a potsherd or, in fact, from anything else. Then the enormous variety of design in itself makes it extremely improbable that each pattern is a copy of an actual Sikyatki piece, the pattern of which is carried in the mind of the potter. The number of fragments giving any idea of the original pattern that can be gathered at Sikyatki in the course of an afternoon is very small, — half a dozen if you are lucky, and these but fragmentary. Some of these will be in the angular type not at present favored by the Hopi, others will be crude.

Collecting ancient pottery designs is a laborious and time consuming process, as any archaeologist will agree. Anyone who is acquainted with the hasty way in which pottery is turned out commercially on the First Mesa must be extremely skeptical of the existence of a separate and authentic Sikyatki prototype for each of the great variety of modern designs. Furthermore, the unsatisfactory character of most of the Sikyatki fragments make it necessary for the artist to make plentiful use of her own inventive faculties and her feeling for style in reconstructing the pattern. I have myself picked up a considerable number of sherds from the surface of the Sikyatki mound, and I have seen in the houses of First Mesa the sherds from which the potter claims to derive their patterns, and there were none that would not impose this requirement upon the artist. That the artists themselves recognize this may be seen by turning once more to their own statements. All women speak of "studying out the line of the design;" that is, reconstructing the design on the basis of their own knowledge and sensitiveness to form. Nampeyo, who was the founder of the Sikyatki school of ceramics,

and who is still its leading representative, says further, "When I first began to paint, I used to go to the ancient village and pick up pieces of pottery and copy the designs. That is how I learned to paint. But now I just close my eyes and see designs and I paint them." Of the personal characteristics of Nampeyo's style, we shall speak at another place. It is sufficient to say here that the patterns she sees now are not the Sikyatki patterns which she used in her youth, although they are quite within the range of the Sikyatki style. We have already mentioned the fact that modern women dream designs in the best Sikyatki manner.

These circumstances, coupled with observations on the working methods of the Hopi potters, lead to the conclusion that women are no longer dependent on ancient pottery for their ideas. They still sometimes use ancient sherds as a starting point for new designs, but even in the reconstructions there is the opportunity and indeed necessity for a considerable amount of free invention. The fluency of artists in the Sikyatki style is ample proof of its complete assimilation.

Hopi pottery is made commercially with the greatest economy of time. For the most part small pieces are made and enough clay is gathered at one time to make a dozen or more pots. These are molded and set aside to dry and then all are polished and painted together. These factory methods, together with the fact that the trader, himself a Hopi, will buy anything and throw away whatever is too poor for sale, rather than demand better work, combine to produce the worst possible workmanship. The paste is soft, — it can often be scratched with the finger nail, — the pigments are badly prepared and carelessly applied so that the colors soon rub off, the vessels are underfired and the fires are so carelessly built that smudging of the vessels almost invariably results. It is all the more surprising, in view of these low standards of workmanship, that the decorative vitality of the work should have remained unimpaired. In spite of the hastiness of the workmanship, there is no endless repetition of stereotyped patterns, but an unfailing freshness and variety of design. Since, as we have seen, this endless variety of designs is not copied from Sikyatki prototypes, we must conclude that this surprising exuberance is due to the very high development of the inventive faculty among the Hopi women. These potters constantly invent new patterns, or rather new variants of typical Sikyatki patterns, because it is as easy as painting the old ones and very much more enjoyable. When we compare this vitality with the artistic sterility that immediately preceded it, we conclude that inventiveness is not a peculiarly Hopi gift of mind, but rather that the introduction of a new medium of expression released an apparently inexhaustible stream of artistic creativeness which found no outlet in the old cramped style. Through some such stimulus it may yet be possible to revive ceramic art in those villages where it is nearing extinction through its own barrenness.

Although copying from archaic pottery plays no noticeable part in the development of decorative styles outside of the Hopi, it is not entirely unknown in other places. One Zuni woman spoke of hunting for ancient potsherds near her farm and using the designs thus discovered; and at Acoma the work of several women shows evidence of having been similarly inspired by the black and white ware of that district, although no one spoke of digging for sherds. It was also an important factor in the revival of painted ware at San Ildefonso that preceded the present dominance of polished wares. Imitation of the antique no longer plays any role in that pueblo.

There is everywhere a considerable amount of conscious borrowing of designs among villages. In this respect Zuni is exceptional; no Zuni woman will admit copying a design from another pueblo. This is wholly consistent with the low regard in which the Zunis hold their neighbors. Nevertheless, I saw one Zuni jar which showed more than a little Acoma influence even to the laying out of the field, which was completely at variance with the Zuni pattern. The pot had been made at Zuni by a Zuni woman, but the design was obviously borrowed. I saw several examples of this pattern in one household at Zuni, and have since seen the design in various collections, — always repeated in exactly the same form. Hopi pottery is everywhere greatly admired, and Hopi designs are in common use at San Ildefonso, where their introduction is credited to Julian Martinez, the husband of the famous Maria. Zuni pottery is well thought of at Acoma and Laguna, and many Zuni designs are current at the latter village where their origin is fully recognized. At Laguna I saw a pot of typical Zuni feeling and treatment, which I first took to be a Zuni pot. My informant, however, assured me that at was an old Laguna piece. Later she remembered that it had been made by her uncle, one of the last men-women of Laguna, a famous potter, now dead, who had once visited Zuni and had been so much impressed by Zuni pottery that he introduced the deer and other typical designs into Laguna. A number of typical Zuni designs are current in Acoma, but the Acomas claim to have originated them. The claim is by no means valid. The designs are traditional at Zuni, but are found only on comparatively recent Acoma pots.

One woman in Santo Domingo owned a pattern book, a series of photographs of several hundred traditional Santo Domingo designs which she had drawn for the museum of Santa Fé. At First Mesa one woman showed me a copy of Fewkes' second Sikyatki volume, which she had recently received as a gift from a white visitor. She said that she often consulted it in planning her designs, but as she has had it for only two years and has been making pottery for very much longer, it has probably had no great influence on her work. Julian Martinez, who more than any other one person has influenced San Ildefonso decorative style, has a notebook which he has kept for many years, in which he notes designs which appeal to him. He has worked in the Santa Fé museum and at various archaeological diggings, and the material in his notebook is derived from the most diverse ancient and modern sources. I could not see

in his work any utilization of this vast erudi-
tion. Of all pots made at San Ildefonso, Julian's exhibit the simplest designs, sometimes
only a row of scallops or dots around the rim
of a large bowl, executed with such exquisite
technical perfection, and such an unerring
sense of the limitations and possibilities of
his technique that his products are incomparably finer than anything else produced in
San Ildefonso, or, indeed, in the whole Southwest. For these he needs no patternbook, no
poring over the archaeologists' tray of
sherds. He has created a style in which he
can operate blindly, feeling his way like a
cat in the dark.

I could not find any trace of deliberate
copying of the decoration of articles of white
manufacture, such as is found, for instance
among the Navajo, who copy the patterns of
brightly colored commercial blankets, or the
Northwest basket makers who use calico designs. The influence of the white man is more
subtle and destructive. Pottery is manufactured for sale to white tourists, and the Indian potter makes what the trader tells her
the white man wants. Under this influence
she makes abominations like candle-sticks
and contorted vases. But by far the most
common pieces are diminutive copies of aboriginal forms which are still decorated in the
pure native style. Even at Laguna where
disintegration has gone farthest, excellent
pieces of this type are still occasionally made.
However, the mistaken policy of school teachers who teach growing girls to draw cows and
chickens in the style of white kindergartens,
telling them that this is "art," is bound to
destroy all feeling for decorative form in the
younger generation.

It might further be remarked that there
does not seem to be any inclination to derive
ornament directly from other objective
sources. Although some few plant and animal
forms are more or less realistically represented and certain natural phenomena symbolically, the artist in search of an original
design does not ordinarily look for it in the
patterning of the rattlesnake or configuration
of the corn plant.

After this brief consideration of the sources
of decorative material, we have now to consider other factors which may influence the
choice of design.

Criticism

In the foregoing chapter, in which the attempt has been made to formulate the principles of design according to which pottery is
fashioned, we have had occasion to call attention to certain general standards of taste,
expressed and unexpressed, to which the artistic product conforms. These are concerned
largely with the laying out of the field, the
ratio of design to background, the use of col-
or, number preferences, and similar matters.
These are general standards, and it is in the
light of these canons of taste that the following more purely personal criticisms and reactions must be considered.

A considerable amount of variation is observed in the reactions of different individuals to new ideas of decoration. Everywhere
I went women were interested in seeing the
photographic material which I had with
me. Often the news that I had pictures
of pots preceded me, and women asked immediately to see the pictures. Most of the
pictures were greeted with a chorus of admiration from the women, and all their children, as well as any other members of the
family or neighbors who happened to be in
the house. The interest and admiration were
not confined to the female members. Men who
would scarcely look at pottery their wives
were making would all gather around to see
the pictures. However, the degree and quality
of their interest varied all the way from the
general curiosity which all Indians have for
any kind of pictures to a professional interest
in the various types of design and the technical skill displayed.

Acoma women, on the whole, were not much
interested in pictures. They examined them
without comment, did not show any marked
preferences, and had no criticisms to offer.

At Zuni requests for criticisms were fruitful, but this, I think, was due not so much to
the more critical attitude of the Zuni women

as to the fact that I happened to have with me a large amount of Zuni material. On the whole, the women were very much more interested in these Zuni pictures than in material from other pueblos. The women differed very much among themselves in their reactions. The woman who in other respects was my best informant said little of interest in regard to the pictures, other than to name such of the designs as she knew, and in some cases to state whether she liked the design or not. As a rule, her only comment was, "I don't like that," or "That is nice." But in some cases she ventured to criticise the drawing. The deer on one jar "looked like pigs;" another jar was condemned as uneven; several were called "funny." Criticisms from other informants were of about the same character. "The deer look like rabbits." "The deer house is drawn wrong." "Someone did not know how to draw deer and put spirals there instead. This design should have deer." "Deer are not good for the inside of a bowl." "Dirty looking," (of a jar covered with geometric designs, making liberal use of black paint). On the whole, however, the women found more to admire than to criticise in the collection. Sometimes special plates were singled out for admiration, and the potter would study the design carefully, with a view to making it. She would always return to her first love for another look after all the other pictures had been examined.

Quite a different attitude prevailed in regard to designs from other pueblos. The women looked at them all as curiosities, and were highly amused at some of them. The bird patterns of Laguna and Sia were regarded as utterly fantastic and aroused considerable mirth. There was no inclination to reproduce such freakish objects. The most generally admired were the strictly geometric patterns of the Santo Domingo ware, notwithstanding that the Zuni women on the whole found the shape of these vessels unpleasing. Some women asked for copies of these photographs. The old San Ildefonso pottery aroused no comment, favorable or otherwise. It is, of course, less striking than the other types. I had no photographs of Hopi pottery. Some of the women said, quite without conviction, that they would like to make one or the other of the designs pictured, generally adding, "But I don't think I could draw it like that." I do not believe that any of them had any very serious intention of using any of the designs shown, except perhaps one who, at my request, adapted one of the Santo Domingo patterns, which she admired, to a Zuni jar. She was sufficiently pleased with the result to want to repeat the design. However, the character of the design had been so altered to fit the Zuni ideas of value, that it was quite unrecognizable in its adapted form.

This is quite different from the attitude of Hopi women who are remarkably receptive to new ideas. They had a most professional interest in the pictures, looking at them always with the primary object of seeing what they could use in their own work. Their comments were singularly unilluminating, although their reactions were very decided. They quickly singled out the designs that interested them, and asked permission to copy them. These designs were then drawn with pencil on paper and put away for future use. I was amazed at the facility with the pencil, and the ease with which they grasped the essentials of the unfamiliar forms. One woman, suffering from the mistaken notion that I was an expert in the handling of the pencil, asked me to copy one design while she did another. I came out badly. She completed two patterns while I was struggling with the intricacies of an interlacing fret.

At San Ildefonso I had a similar experience. The men and women were all much interested in the photographs which I had with me. Julian's reactions were especially notable. He looked over all the pictures with evident interest and enjoyment. Suddenly he took my pencil out of my hand and tore a page from my notebook to copy a bird that struck his fancy. This bird appeared in a narrow border on a Laguna pot and formed an inconspicuous part of the whole design. Other bits of design that he copied for future use were all equally fragmentary. He did not pore over the photographs. He apparently was not interested in new types of decoration or arrangement, but rather in clever little twists that he could embody in his own already highly developed and highly individual style. There seemed to be no doubt in his mind as to what he could and what he could not use. It was this immediate and unhesitating quality in his judgment, and the nature of the material he selected that was especially striking. His remarks were quite unilluminating.

Owing to practical difficulties it was possible in only one instance to get native criticism of local products. It is, naturally, not possible to take one informant into the home of another to criticise her work, and all of my native friends were too polite to give a frank opinion of any pieces of pottery that I had bought. However, at First Mesa, I took one informant to the storeroom of the Hopi trader, ostensibly for the purpose of helping me select pieces for purchase. The trader always has on hand large stocks of native pottery, and I asked my informant to select pieces whose purchase she recommended. Her selection presented the most motley assortment of good and bad painting, some of the pieces being not only unpleasing in design, but also slovenly in workmanship. I soon discovered that the selection was made entirely on the basis of technical excellence of the ware. A handsome bowl by one of Nampeyo's daughters was discarded because one side had a slightly mottled appearance, showing that not all the water had been expelled in the firing. "It will break when you use it." She admitted that the painting was good, but this seemed too unimportant to be commented upon until directly questioned. The prophecy was, alas, correct. I purchased the bowl for the sake of its design, and although I did get it to New York unbroken, it crumbled the first time it was used. She also advised strongly against the purchase of another bowl because it did not ring true, although when questioned, she admitted that this, too, was "pretty."

This emphasis on the technical rather than the artistic qualities of ceramic products is the common pueblo attitude, even in villages, like those of First Mesa, where pottery is no longer made for household use. Everywhere when potters were asked what they considered most important in their art, they spoke of avoiding cracks in the coiling, the elimination of particles of dirt that would cause the vessel to crack in firing, care in the building of the fire, so that the vessels would not be broken by uneven firing or smudged by proximity to the fuel. Other things frequently mentioned were symmetrical modelling and careful finishing of the rim. Design was mentioned only incidentally. That this attitude towards technical standards should still prevail among the Hopi, where such extreme degeneration of technique has taken place, is striking evidence of its importance and tenacity.

Instruction

Methods of instruction show the same preoccupation with technical excellence. From a Zuni woman I received the following account of how she would teach a young girl:

When a girl starts to make a jar, I should tell her to take a handful of clay about the size of a cup, and to work it in her hands, using two fingers, until it is like a cup. Then she should put it in a mold and roll strips of clay about as thick as her thumb and about two or three feet long. She should use about five such strips, smoothing them all the time with the gourd scraper, and then she should put on two shorter strips to make the top. She must make it even around the lips and cut it off with a string, or pinch it with her fingers and cut off the extra clay to make a clean edge. She must not make the mouth too small like the Hopi jars, because it is too hard to get the gourd dipper in and out. She will not be able to make a good shape at first. Sometimes it will tip over on one side. But afterwards, she will learn to do it so that it is even all around.

Then I should tell the girl to soak the white clay for the white paint. She should put it in a bowl of water and let it soak so that it is smooth. Then she should see if it is thick enough. When it sticks to her fingers and drops off slowly, it is right. Then she should mix the black paint. She should rub the black stone in water. She must rub it hard because if it is not rubbed enough, it will not be a true black. She must add something to it, sugar or the boiled juice of the yucca to make it fast. Then she should mix the red paint. Then everything is ready.

Then I should teach the girl to measure the jar with her hands, so that the design will come out even. First she should measure around the top. For a small jar the designs should be about two finger widths apart, for a full size water jar, about a span. I should tell her to mark with her finger-nail the place where the designs will come. Then she should measure down from the mouth of the jar. She should mark with her nail how far up the mold comes, and that much will remain unpainted. She should use about four or five large designs and smaller ones in between to fill out. The jar must be covered all over, but there should be plenty of white showing. I should tell her not to use too many small designs, because then it is too black and that is not nice. She should use mostly black paint and only a little bit of red.

I should not tell her what to paint, but she will know. When I was a girl, I watched my mother making pottery and learned how it do it. It is hard to learn how to paint well, — harder than making the pot.

From San Ildefonso comes the following account:

If I were teaching a young girl, I should tell her that she must be most careful with the polishing, — not to scratch the pot and to make it nice and smooth. I would tell her how to make the shape. I would tell her to make any shape she likes and I would show her how to fix it nice and smooth. I would tell her to be careful of the mouth, and to fix it smooth and fine and even all around. She should be careful with the polishing, not to scratch the surface and not to use too much grease, because then it will not dry thoroughly.

In painting I should tell her to use her own brain and to paint any kind of design she likes, whatever she can think of. I should not tell her what to put on, but I should say to her: "Use your own brain and paint anything you like, only put it on straight and even." She would learn the different designs by watching the other women paint and by using her own brain and making the kind she wants. I make designs out of my head, — things that I have never seen before.

At San Ildefonso I received instruction in pottery making from a number of different women. The methods of all were similar, and probably not very different from those used in teaching young people of their own race. After the clay was carefully mixed and cleaned and kneaded to the satisfaction of the teacher, I was given a mold, shown how to handle the clay and told, "Go ahead and make." — "What shall I make?" — "Anything you like. We make all different kinds. Make any kind you want." After the walls were built up, I was instructed in the use of the scraper, being told to work from the inside and outside, but still nothing definite in regard to form. "The girls watch us make, and then when they want to make their own, they make anything they want." When the half finished vessel was presented for criticism, my teacher pointed out the weak places in the walls, the bad line where the walls joined the bottom, asymmetries and irregularity of the rim, but there was no criticism of the form as such. Occasionally I was told to work at the inside, that is, push the walls out to make a rounder shape, but that is all.

Great pains were expended in showing me how to finish the vessel before polishing it. The vessel was scraped with a knife to make a very smooth surface, and it was a long time before I finished this to the satisfaction of my teacher. This was true also of the polishing which had to be done over and over before a sufficiently high, even polish was attained. Whenever I scratched a vessel, or produced a pebbled surface by too vigorous use of the polishing stone while the vessel was still damp, I was told to do it over, beginning with a fresh slip of red clay.

When we started to paint, I was told once more to paint whatever I wished. When I insisted on more definite instructions, one woman, though amazed at my stupidity, said she would paint one of her bowls while I did mine, copying her design, stroke by stroke as she made it. Another woman began my bowl for me, starting a row of scallops around the rim and telling me to continue the same way. On another pot she made the first of two paired designs, and told me to finish according to this pattern. The third woman did this for my first pot, but refused all help after that. "You must think yourself what you want to paint. That is the way we do."

The Hopi women also follow the same plan of instruction. Great care was taken to make me understand the technical processes of molding, finishing and polishing, and my teachers were exacting taskmasters in all these matters. But I was left to my own devices in the matter of painting. Here, too, one woman painted a dish and had me copy it as she worked. Another brought me a book containing pictures of Sikyatki pottery and told me to copy any one I wished. By another I was told to "make a design out of your head." I obediently went ahead, trying as the native learner does, to create a design in keeping with prevailing taste without actually copying anything seen or remembered. I managed fairly well for a shallow bowl, a peculiar Hopi product. The Hopi style of painting had already become associated with this form of vessel in my mind, and the result, while not copied, would pass as very bad Hopi design. But I had no success when it came to painting a band around a small round jar. This is not a common Hopi type of vessel, although it is common at San Ildefonso, and the design which I found myself making was a typical San Ildefonso panelled border. The design was not one which I had made, nor even one that I had seen, but the whole arrangement of motives was characteristic of the San Ildefonso ware. Apparently in even so short a period of observation and imitation (ten days), I had assimilated the San Ildefonso style to such an extent that I unconsciously reproduced it when confronted by a vessel of the familiar proportions. It must be by some such process as this that the traditional styles are passed on.

The Range of Variability

The number of designs which the artist has at her command varies considerably from place to place and from individual to individual. We have already seen that the four types of pottery under discussion show very great differences in variability. The variability of any style seems to be in some measure correlated with the number of individuals in the village who engage in the manufacture of pottery. At Zuni although most of the older women know how to make pottery, few of them, and none of the younger women, will now take the trouble to make what is required for their household needs. Where lard tins have not displaced native pottery, they prefer to buy what they need from one of the few women who engages in this occupation on a semi-professional basis. Zuni pottery has never been exploited by the traders and therefore is not profitable for the general population. However, for a few older women who supply the needs of the pueblo the manufacture of pottery is an important source of income. I had an opportunity to visit three such women. Two of these had a considerable number of jars completed and ready for sale, and among them the proportion of duplication was high. Each one seemed to have a favorite design which she repeated over and over again, to the exclusion of other patterns. With one it was the familiar deer and sunflower pattern, with the other, the diagonal pattern of Acoma inspiration to which we have referred before. The third professional potter had no completed jars, but she had in various stages of work a considerable number of pieces of different sizes and shapes. Work on pottery goes forward slowly in midsummer, and in the summer of 1924 the ravages of a whooping cough epidemic still further impeded the progress of women's work, so I had to leave Zuni before any of these pieces were completed, and I never saw what designs were painted on them. However, I did see my informant copying on one of her bowls the design of a bowl which she had made a number of years ago, and which was in use in her household. From this I infer that her methods were not very different from those of the other women who make pottery for a living. It is another contradiction between theory and practice. It is, however, significant that the stock in trade of any one of these professional potters showed less variety in design than the pieces in use in her own household.

This lends further support to the opinion already expressed that repetition of designs is resorted to as an expedient made necessary by the poverty of the imagination, but that it is not by any means a deliberate esthetic choice.[3]

In spite of the tendency of professional potters to specialize in one or another type of design, most of the designs that are still in use are the common knowledge of all the potters, and all the potters can and do use all the more popular patterns. This seems to be particularly true of the non-professional potters who still have in their possession pieces of their own manufacture which show considerable variety of design. These generally included a few unsuccessful pieces which seemed to me to fall short of the best Zuni standards and which my interpreter (not herself a potter) would tell me in confidence, and without my suggestion were "not very good." My collection of Zuni designs was secured too late for me to be able to get any definite data on the actual number of these patterns known to each of my informants, but my impression, gained from a survey of household pottery, is that there is no very great difference between individuals in this respect. This, it must be understood, applies only to "new," i. e. current designs, which form only a portion of the collection. I doubt very much that the obsolete designs are so widely known. My informant had a reputation

[3] The conclusions in regard to Zuni are put forward tentatively and with considerable hesitation. It is possible to live in Zuni in complete ignorance of what is going on. Judging from the number of burnings, there certainly seemed to be little pottery making going on during the summer of 1924, but whether this was due to the season or to some other causes or was the usual condition, is hard to say. My interpreter on whom I depended for introductions after visiting six or seven women told me these are all who "knew how." With the exception of the three professionals, none of these had work in hand. That these were the only potters may have been true,—probably not. Some women refused to receive me; undoubtedly my interpreter was averse to sponsoring me outside her immediate circle, and for obvious economic reasons wished to have me work as much as possble within her own immediate family. Her mother was my best informant. Such considerations make it difficult to find out even so simple a fact as how many women make pottery.

for unusual knowledge among the white residents of Zuni. Of course, among the Zunis themselves each woman considered herself the greatest repository of ancient lore. However, I cannot believe that this woman's truly remarkable memory is shared by her compatriots. It must be remembered that the life of pottery at Zuni is comparatively short. A pot that has lived through five or six years of daily trips to the spring is considered of respectable age by the owner. Moreover, the pueblo has been very carefully combed by collectors for old pieces. I was fortunate enough to secure one very fine old piece. My informant saw it in my room and asked to borrow it so that she might study the design. A somewhat garbled version of this pattern appears as No. 46 of the series. That my informant had not already included this design, leads me to infer that the collection represents only designs which she herself actually used.

We have already had occasion to note the great variability of design at Acoma and on the First Mesa where pottery making is one of the important industries of the village and engages the activity of practically all of the women. The professionalism of Acoma and Hopi pottery making is of an entirely different character than that of Zuni. We have already spoken of the apparently inexhaustible inventiveness of the Hopi potters. The same thing occurs at Isleta. Here the women specialize in very small pieces which are sold at the railway station at Albuquerque. The characteristic Isleta style is a sort of simplified Acoma. I spent all afternoon watching three women decorate little baskets about four inches in diameter. The women talked and laughed among themselves and certainly did not appear to be concentrating all their thoughts on their artistic labors. Nevertheless in the course of less than two hours the three of them completed about forty-two pieces, no two of which were alike. These "pottery bees" are a common feature of Hopi social life. If a woman sits down in her front room to decorate pottery, it generally follows that a relative or neighbor who also has pottery to decorate will bring over her work and join her. Three or four women will frequently gather in this way and gossip merrily over their work. It may be that there is some vitalizing force in this interchange of gossip and ideas at the same time that is reflected in the vigor of the art. However, too much importance must not be given to this idea. At Acoma, where the art is equally lively "pottery bees" are not the rule. Pottery is mostly made in summer at Acomita, a straggling farming village that is not at all conducive to social activities of this kind.

At Laguna, however, the situation is quite different. Here we have a dying art, now uttering its last feeble gasps. It has succumbed to commercialism, complicated by the removal of the market when the Santa Fé railroad removed its tracks and built a new station three miles from the pueblo. The women are all hopeless about the state of their art. They would say "We don't make good pottery here any longer. Why don't you go to Acoma? When we want pottery, we buy it from the Acomas." A few women still make small pieces which they peddle on the road, but not only are they inferior in workmanship, but the old style has completely disintegrated, and the products show a wearisome repetition of a few elements without any apparent sense of order or of style.

These facts would seem to indicate some sort of relation between the number of individuals engaged in pottery making and the vigor and variety of the style. I am of the opinion that such a connection does exist, but I do not believe that this explains entirely the difference in variability between, say, the Zuni and Hopi decorative styles. In connection with this problem I have gone over the Stevenson collection of Zuni ware in the United States National Museum. This collection was made in 1879-1880, when pottery making was still a household art engaged in as necessity arose by all the women. The collection contains more pieces than I saw at Zuni in the summer of 1924, more, probably, than

are now to be found at Zuni, and therefore might be expected to show more different styles. It is decidedly more variable than the present product, but still duplication is not at all uncommon. One would never feel that it shows striking originality on the part of the artists whose work is represented. The difference in variability between the old and the contemporary Zuni pottery might very well be due to a concentration of the art in the hands of a few individuals. However, when we compare a number of these old Zuni jars, selected at random from the Stevenson collection, with an equal number of Acoma jars of the same period, and therefore probably made under similar conditions, we find an infinitely greater range of variety in the Acoma product, which must be due to something inherent in the style. In any comparison of this kind we must bear in mind that the population of Acoma has always been much smaller than that of Zuni, and that, therefore, any collection from Acoma must be drawn from a narrower field.

A still more striking instance is the difference of the present Hopi ware from what immediately preceded it. At the end of the nineteenth century the ceramic product of the Hopi was a whitish pottery closely resembling the present ware of the Zuni. Many of the same decorative units were used, and the same formal arrangement was adhered to and, as at Zuni, the pottery tended to become stereotyped. The variability of the present ware is truly extraordinary. Yet the two products come from the same village, in many cases from the same individuals. The potter working in one style produced a stereotyped and commonplace object, and in another an original and individual design. We must therefore, recognize that there is something inherent in the decorative style that encourages or inhibits originality, irrespective of the endowment of the particular artist.

Individuality in Design

Although the women do not recognize any very definite proprietorship in designs, every potter claims that she can distinguish readily between the work of her fellow artists. "I can always tell by looking at a jar who made it." "All the women use different designs."— "All the women paint differently." One Zuni woman was more explicit: "If I painted my bowls like every one else, I might lose my bowl when I took dinner to the dancers in the plaza.[4] I am the only person who makes a checkerboard design around the rim, so I can always tell my bowl by looking at the edge. I don't have to use any mark on my bowl because I recognize the design." At Laguna one woman while looking over my photographs stated that one of the bowls pictured had been made by her aunt. "My aunt always made designs like that."

The Indian trader at Polacca who handles the entire output of Hopi pottery can name the maker of almost any one of the several hundred pieces of pottery in his storeroom. Every day women bring in their work, and every day large shipments are sent away. Women will trade a lot of a dozen or more pieces of pottery for credit at the store, and the pottery is generally sold in job lots. No stock record is kept; in fact, no record of any kind. It seems impossible that the trader should be able to remember the identity of each piece. He claims that he can tell the maker from the style of decoration, and I do not question that this is probably true.

During the summer of 1925 I visited this store with one of the best potters of Hano in order to test her ability to distinguish individual work. This woman works all day at the Polacca day school. She has very heavy family responsibilities; the demands upon her time, coupled with the usual snobbishness of members of aristocratic pueblo families keep her from visiting a great deal in the village. Therefore she was probably seeing these particular pieces of pottery for the first time. No attempt was made to identify the large

number of small and badly made pieces, but she was able to tell the name of the makers of almost all the larger and more striking pieces. She would frequently turn to the trader for corroboration of her guess, and he almost invariably agreed with her.

My own attempts along this line were rather disappointing. At Zuni I was quite unable to find any noticeable difference in style in the work of different individuals. The work of the professional potters showed a more perfect mastery of technique than the general run of Zuni pottery; the vessels were better formed, and more accurately painted, but they were not distinguished by individuality of style. However, the material is so scattered that not much along this particular line can be gathered. There is no validity in a comparison of general impressions of objects seen at different times. The style is so formal that personal peculiarities of style would be displayed in minute variations only. Because contemporary material is unavailable for any comparison of this kind, I went over the Stevenson material in the United States National Museum for this particular point. Any collection of this size made within a single year is bound to be representative of the general type of the pueblo. In all probability it contains several specimens from each of the active potters. Unfortunately there was not time to make an exhaustive study of this interesting collection, but even a hasty survey brought to light some rather interesting facts. In the first place, the collection is obviously the work of many hands. All degrees of technical skill are shown, ranging from crudely modelled and painted pieces to jars that exhibit a very high standard of technical excellence, brushwork and surface polish being superior to anything found in Zuni today. We can be reasonably sure that the best and worst are the work of different potters. A classification of the material according to technical standards would give a rough apportionment of the work among groups of potters of varying skill. This would, however, be only a very rough division. I have found that potters are

[4] At Zuni masked dances start in the morning and continue until sundown. The dancers come out and dance in the plaza in the morning and then return to the kiva until the afternoon ceremonies. During this interval the wives of the members of the organization which is presenting the ceremony, bring bowls of cooked food for the mid-day meal of the participants.

not equally successful with all their pieces. Nevertheless a woman who is expert with a brush will always produce neat, sharply drawn patterns, even if certain of her designs fail to please because of faulty planning. There are also certain minor features of drawing, such as whether the deer is long and thin or short and fat; the type of tail on a bird, etc., that set off the work of one potter from that of another. However, I should not hazard any inference of this kind on the basis of design content or arrangement except that it is probable that the freer forms of composition are not from the brush of the same artist that made the jars executed in more constrained style. For we must remember that although the general type was more variable at that period, there was even then a tendency to repeat certain fixed forms.

There is more satisfactory evidence on the positive side of the problem. There are a number of cases in which it is possible to say of two or three jars that we are unquestionably dealing with the work of a single individual. Two jars were as like as two peas, and differed so completely from the accepted Zuni style both in form and ornament that there cannot be the slightest doubt that they were made by one person of an experimental turn of mind. In another case three jars were all decorated with design No. 5, of the modern series. Of these, two were executed with fine line work so incomparably superior to the average Zuni product that here too we must postulate a single worker. Another pattern is represented by several examples which, in the plentiful use of paint, are quite unlike anything else, and which, therefore, are probably the work of a single artist. In this as in the preceding case, the pots, although very different from other Zuni ware, show an exceptionally close similarity to one another. There are other examples which are put forward with less assurance where several pots have similar designs, designs which, while thoroughly in keeping with the Zuni style, are yet distinctive, and which for no apparent reason have become obsolete. If these designs were associated with individual potters, we would

have in the death of the inventor an explanation of the extinction of the pattern. Designs of this kind are seen in Pl. IV, f, V, a. I have refrained from drawing any inferences from examples in Pl. XX (p. 77), both of which are very distinctive, and each of which is represented by several examples, because these appear to me so archaic that they may well represent an earlier style and not a contemporary variation. Pl. V, b, is also undoubtedly ancient. There are a number of vessels of this type, two in the National Museum, one in a private collection in Santa Fé, and one in Dr. Kidder's collection, — all different in design, yet all showing the same distinguishing characteristics. All three pieces have a peculiar form, almost globular, a remarkably high polish that is found nowhere else in Zuni pottery, singularly fine linework, and other more elusive traits. These three pieces may not be contemporaneous with the rest of the collection, but whatever their age, they are undoubtedly the work of a single rarely gifted individual. There are also a number of freak pieces, unique in the National Museum collection, which, however, may be matched elsewhere. Plate IV, d, for instance, is found also in the American Museum of Natural History, and probably both come from the same maker.

It is possible to multiply examples of this kind, but they are not very significant. The evidence of strong individualism in painting is wanting in Zuni. It would seem that in 1879 skill in pottery making and knowledge of design were rather evenly distributed among the women of the pueblo.

At San Ildefonso individualism has in some ways reached its highest development. All the more expert potters are known by name to traders and collectors in Santa Fé and elsewhere. A number of them, in fact, are so well known that they sign their names to all their products. The name is frequently misleading. By no means all of the pottery that goes under Maria Martinez' name is hers. Much of it she has modelled; some of it is modelled by her two sisters; and practically all is painted by her husband, Julian. However, the work turned out by this family is all of surpassing excellence. The same is true also of the work of Tonita, whose pots are, for the most part, decorated by her husband, Juan Cruz. Their work is almost as good as that of the Martinez family. Julian's designs are, on the whole, simpler than Juan's. Some, which are the last word in brevity of expression, are unmistakable. These excepted, it is not easy to tell the work of the two families apart. Both are flawless in technique. I have frequently been mistaken in assigning particular pieces to one or the other house. But between these two families and the rest of the San Ildefonso potters no confusion is possible. The distinction, however, is one of technique, rather than style. No other women besides Maria and Tonita seem to achieve the deep lustre of polished jet which characterizes the finish of bowls of their workmanship. Then there is an almost mechanical perfection in painting that is not found in the work of other women. No one else achieves the distinction of Julian at his best, but aside from this, the ware is fairly uniform stylistically. This, indeed, might be expected in an art where ornament as such is completely subordinated to perfection of technique and beauty of finsh.

Dr. Guthe reports as follows, in regard to the individual differences of his three principal informants at San Ildefonso at the time when these women were making polychrome pottery:

The type of design used by any one potter expresses her personality. The type of design used by any one potter is very constant, and is distinctly individual. It is a comparatively easy matter, by inspection of the design alone, to distinguish the vessels made by different potters.

The designs are planned in several different ways. Maria Martinez sits with the bowl in her hands a few moments, doing nothing; apparently she is working out in her mind the combination of elements she will use. Designs so conceived are generally simple. Maximiliana Martinez begins painting almost at once. While she is working, ideas occur to her and are incorporated. Occasionally after the painting has been completed, and the vessel set aside, she will pick it up again to add some detail. This method of working is apt to cause some-

what involved figures. Antonita Roybal, in choosing her designs, refers to drawings of her own, or to photographs which have come into her hands, of San Ildefonso vessels. This potter uses a pencil to outline very sketchily the design upon the vessel, as an aid in obtaining proper symmetry. The figures obtained in this manner are usually elaborate.

This was written while the old polychrome pottery was the only ware made at San Ildefonso. Possibly the fact that this has since been displaced by polished wares with simpler decoration, accounts for the fact that I noted no such striking difference as Guthe records in the work of these three potters.

In the Acoma and Hopi styles which are generally more variable, one might expect to find a more marked development of individuality in painting. Unfortunately there is not enough contemporaneous pottery in any one place to make an intensive study of this kind. However, I know two Acoma potters whose work is absolutely unmistakable. One makes an entirely black on white pottery, apparently influenced by archaic patterns, using interlocking spirals as the basis of her design, the only instance of the use of a true spiral. The other woman decorates in an infinite variety of patterns. She makes pots of archaic form, with ancient black and white designs with interlocking key figures. She also uses designs more nearly like the current Acoma type. But in this style she over-reaches herself. She makes a most unorthodox use of familiar bird motives; the exuberance and complexity of design is so great that it eludes analysis. It certainly has little in common with the forms in which Acoma design is generally cast. I have found this pottery in the museums and shops of Santa Fé, and in private collections as far away as New York, and always it is as unmistakable as if it were signed with the maker's name. This woman is well known in Santa Fé, and in many cases there I was able to verify my guess.

The same thing is true also of Hopi work. In the short time I spent on First Mesa, I learned to distinguish the work of three potters. The work of Nampeyo and her daughters, for instance, is quite unmistakable. She makes no modern white forms, no worthless trifles. She makes only dignified pieces in the best traditional style. Technically, her work is superior to that of any other Hopi potter.[5] Her vessels are more symmetrically and gracefully molded with great subtlety of line in the flare of the lips. Her designs are executed with greater delicacy and precision, and her line work is superior to that of her fellow workers. Furthermore, her designs are of a different character. There is less design per square inch of pot. At times her patterns are almost impressionistic in their economy.

Another woman, to whom we have referred before, uses only angular designs of the pre-Sikyatki period, frets and bands excellently drawn. She prefers a white slip, and encouraged by the trader, makes flat plates. A third woman specializes in high vases copied after products of white inspiration, to which she cleverly adapts a great variety of Sikyatki designs, various broad bands and the crescent shaped bird forms, here elongated into a kind of crook. I do not doubt that the shelves of the trader contain specimens of a number of

[5] I refer here only to artistic technique, not to the quality of the ware, the paints or the methods of firing, which, like all Hopi work, are abominable.

equally individualistic styles, and that as familiarity with style increases, more personalities will disengage themselves from the general mass. Of course, not every woman has the magic touch. Below the mere handful of creative artists is a dead level of unoriginal mediocrity. These second raters produce pottery that is frequently well made and pleasing in design, but which is nevertheless utterly lacking in distinction. But in spite of this thoroughly human preponderance of mediocrity, there is a goodly sprinkling of artists of marked individuality. It seems rather doubtful that the natural endowment is very much greater than among the Zunis. Certainly twenty-five years ago Hopi potters did not display striking originality. These same women, or their daughters, painting twenty-five years later in a different decorative style, produced work of notable individuality. This is another aspect of the problem of variability within a given style. At Zuni, where the style is generally uniform, individual differences are shown mainly in the mastery of technique, but with the increased variability of design goes the tendency toward the development of distinctive styles in the hands of gifted individuals.

V

SYMBOLISM

The table in Appendix I gives the names and interpretations of the set of Zuni designs shown in the accompanying plates. These designs were drawn for me by an old Zuni woman, an excellent potter who has been practicing her art for at least forty years. She is, moreover, the head of one of the priestly families of Zuni, the guardian of one of the most important medicine bundles of the tribe. She was an able informant on all matters of religious belief and practice, knew many esoteric ceremonies and imparted freely whatever she knew. If, therefore, there is any esoteric symbolism in Zuni pottery designs, as has been claimed by Cushing [1] and others, this information could be secured from this woman.

She told me that every design is significant. It has a name and a "story." Its reference is to a situation or an event rather than an object or an idea. The designs were presented to her twice for identification, once right after they were drawn in 1924, again after the passage of a year, and the two sets of interpretations are given in adjacent columns.

We have discussed in another place [2] the character of the names. They are not pattern names, since they are so loosely applied that there is no definite association between any name and a particular form. The same name is applied to elements having nothing in common from a stylistic point of view, and conversely, the same element may be differently designated in different contexts. Nor are the designs symbols in any sense of the word.

[1] Cushing, 1886.
[2] See p. 53 f.

We are justified in using the word symbol only where the association between the design and the object or idea suggested is fixed and recognized. Zuni designs, with their shifting meanings are neither tribal nor individual symbols.

The patterns on meal bowls are, in a sense, symbolic. They are realistic or conventionalized but always recognizable representations of certain supernatural beings that figure in mythology and belief in association with springs and standing water. Their use on ceremonial pottery is explained by natives as a kind of compulsive magic. "These are all creatures who frequent springs. If we paint them on our bowls, our bowls will always be full of water like the springs." It is indirect magic, since they are never used on the bowls or jars that are actually used for drawing or storing water. They are employed only on bowls used to hold the sacred cornmeal that is sprinkled as part of every prayer. The use of particular designs on these bowls is part of the rain ritual.

There is, however, one symbol in Zuni art, the "road." This is the line which divides the neck from the body of jars. It is called *onane*, road, the usual Zuni term for the span of life. It is identified not with the life of a being inhabiting the pot, as Cushing claims, but with the life of the potter. For this reason, it is always left unjoined. "When I finish it, I shall finish my road," i. e. end my life. This is a true symbol, the only one in Zuni art. Meal bowl patterns are magical representations.

There is at Zuni one other design which

[69]

might be regarded as a symbol, namely the pattern used on the outer rims of bowls (No. 60). This has been variously interpreted as feathers and prayer-sticks, and the explanation which I heard once is that women paint it on their bowls when they have a prayer, because they do not make prayer-sticks. The designation "feather" is not confined to this design; "prayer-stick," however, is. It is interesting to note that this is one design whose usage is fixed. It is used only on the outside of bowls and its use there is, at the present time, almost obligatory.

In spite of this absence of fixed symbolism, we cannot overlook the tendency at Zuni to invariably associate decorative designs with ideas of a religious character. This is not a personal peculiarity of one woman, but is a general pattern of Zuni thought. At the request of my informant, I did not show the design sketches to other women for their identifications, but whenever I asked the significance of a particular design, I received explanations of a similar character.

Two general types of associations predominate: those concerning the weather, and those concerning the ceremonies for controlling the weather. An overwhelming number of designs suggest clouds of different kinds, — rain, snow, wind, lightning, flowers "because they come out after the rain." Almost all the rest suggest ceremonial paraphernalia, especially the regalia of the masked dancers who figure in the great rain bringing ceremonies. These are the two most important facts in Zuni life. Indeed, it is artificial to make any distinction betwen them. In Zuni ideology the clouds and the masked dancers are one. The interpretations are, therefore, all of one piece. It is an example of the extraordinary pervasiveness of ceremonialism in Zuni life and thought. It is the integrating principle with which all things that make any bid for attention must be related.

The strength of this tendency, coupled with the inconsistency of specific associations, has been interpreted as the last stage in a decaying system of symbolism. It is claimed that these designs were once symbolic and that the knowledge of their significance persists, although the precise meanings have been lost. I cannot see any evidence whatever that this is taking place. There is a definite tendency to associate design, the fluidity of which we have already observed, with the dominating concerns of life. Under the combined influence of the stagnation of art, and the increasing despotism of ritual — two developments which we can observe at Zuni at the present time — this loose association may in time crystallize into fixed symbolism. It may, of course, be the other way round, that it is the increasing fixation of symbolism that causes stagnation. The evidence from other pueblos where design is more fluid, all pointing towards the distinctly secondary nature of interpretations, does not favor this conclusion. But either way, symbolism and rigidity go hand in hand, and Zuni art is not less, but more symbolic today than it was seventy-five years ago.

Among the Hopi the association between designs and objects or ideas is even more tenuous than at Zuni. Here, too, most women will find some significance in designs, when questioned, but the way in which the answer is given indicates that the association is quite secondary, and frequently suggested by the inquirer. These associations, tenuous though they are, are as definitely patterned here as at Zuni. There are no "stories," that is, no complex situations influencing the affairs of man. Nor is any magical potency ever imputed, even secondarily, to designs. Designs, when they have any significance at all, are pictures of material objects. Among these objects topographical features figure prominently. The earth, mountains, rocks, cornfields, houses, and villages are frequently mentioned; also "the sky with clouds and rain," the sun, moon, stars, milky way, and rainbow. Prayersticks and feathers are mentioned but rarely birds, despite obvious resemblances. As at Zuni, there is no consistency in nomenclature, not even within the same pattern. The crescent shaped designs used on bowls are frequently designated "rainbow." Parts of this design are then labelled "belt of her dress'' (this time it was described as ''a female rainbow''), clouds, rain, earth with mountains, cornfields and feathers. There is some tendency to associate red designs with the earth, black with either earth or sky. Unlike Zuni, ceremonial associations are rare, reflecting perhaps, the less important rôle which ceremonialism has been observed to play in Hopi life. Two designs, similar in general outline, were both called ''rainbow'' and later differentiated as male and female. The secondary character of such associations is obvious. We have, moreover, historical data to illuminate the nature of Hopi symbolism. We know under what influences this style of decoration was adopted. There is no reason to assume that the meanings now attached to Sikyatki designs are those originally associated with them, nor is any such claim made by the persons who use them. They adopted and assimilated a fully developed artistic style and reinterpreted it in accordance with their sense of values. Their interpretations, for which they claim only a subjective reality, are strikingly different from those advanced by archaeologists, notably Fewkes.[3] The modern Hopi sees rainbows and mountains where the archaeologist sees birds and serpents. One can take one's choice. Neither can claim to be an explanation of what the design meant to the person who painted it; still less does either throw any real light on the actual origin of the design. These interpretations and the ways in which they are patterned merely reflect the principal interest of the observer. But though they have little value as reconstructions, no one can question their subjective reality.

At Acoma there is no trace whatever of symbolism in design. Even my most communicative informant could give no meanings of any kind. She said, ''We have only three names for designs, red, black and striped. The designs do not mean anything.'' No

amount of questioning elicited any more definite response. It seems very unlikely that this negative evidence is due to reticence.

At San Ildefonso I had a series of designs identified by three different men, all of whom painted pottery, and I have tabulated the results of this inquiry. Not all the men saw all the designs; where no identification is noted, it is because the design was sketched after the interview and not because no name was forthcoming when the design was presented for identification. Here, also, it is generally assumed that designs are significant. The association between name and design is ephemeral, but some association is always found. Here the associations follow individual patterns. To Juan all designs are clouds. Julian shows more imagination; the frequent occurrence of bird designations in his interpretations is notable. When I had these designs identified, I mixed among them certain simple Hopi and Zuni patterns, all drawn on similar slips of paper. The San Ildefonso style is very fluid, and no one seemed surprised to find unfamiliar designs among the collection. They did not recognize them as foreign designs, and although they were unfamiliar, they were named and interpreted along with the rest. There is an association for every design, whether it is familiar or not. The table of San Ildefonso designs is given in Appendix III.

It is clear from all this material that there is at the present time no fixed symbolism in pueblo pottery design, but that, with the exception of Acoma, there is a marked tendency to clothe designs with significance of a purely subjective character. This tendency is no less marked in the styles of recent origin than in the more ancient ones. It is, therefore, not the last relic of a forgotten symbolism, but the psychological basis upon which symbolism might, under suitable conditions, develop. At Zuni there is some tendency for definite meanings to be firmly attached to designs whose usage is fixed.

[3] Fewkes — R. B. A. E. 17, 33.

VI

STABILITY OF DECORATIVE STYLE

The problem of the stability of cultural phenomena may be approached both from the geographical or historical point of view. We may study the variations to which a particular cultural trait is subjected in different places, and from these reconstruct the probable history, or we may endeavor to trace the actual history of special traits within a more restricted field. Of course, the latter method is much to be preferred, and the only reason that it does not figure more largely in anthropological literature is that historical material is so lamentably meager. So many misconceptions are current in regard to the origin and development of decorative forms, — theories based largely on an arbitrary arrangement of co-existent forms in "sequences," — that it is especially important to test the validity of these theories in the light of purely historical data.

As has already been pointed out (p. 4), the Southwest is an especially favorable field for a study of this kind, and I hope in the present chapter to assemble the historical facts which we have concerning ceramic art.

Survey of the History of Pottery in the Southwest

For the purposes of the present study, the history of artistic forms falls into two distinct periods, the modern and the archaeological. The modern period goes back to about 1850,— that is, the period of intimate contact with white civilization. For this period of seventy-five years, large numbers of accurately datable specimens are available for detailed study. Preceding this, and separated from it by a hiatus of some 150 years, is the archaeologi-

cal period. For the period from 1700 to 1850 there is no material, due in large measure to the continuous occupancy of the village sites down to the present day, a condition which naturally makes them unavailable for archaeological investigation. During this period there was no interest in preserving specimens of native art. In 1700 the record is resumed and for 150 years we have easily datable material, going back to the advent of the Spaniards in 1540. Behind this stretches the long prehistoric era, for which we have as yet no absolute time values, but for which we have a great quantity of comparative material and a number of definite chronological sequences.

The archaeological story has received a great deal of attention and is fairly clear, and is every day becoming more thoroughly understood. It is with the development within the very brief mdoern period and more especially within the present generation that the present investigation is concerned. In no one of the four areas here considered has the decorative style stood still, and the extent and nature of the changes have already been hinted at. Nevertheless, it will help our understanding of the problem to review here very briefly the general historical background with special reference to Zuni and Hopi pueblos. This summary is put forward with considerable trepidation by one who is not an archaeologist, and is based principally on Dr. Kidder's conclusions.[1]

Pottery first appears in the southwest in the post-Basket-Maker period. This culture centered in northeastern Arizona. At this

[1] Kidder, 1924.

time the people were living in small units, in semi-subterranean rooms and in caves. They had already been practising agriculture for some time. The pottery of this period was very crude, mostly rough gray ware with no attempt at decoration. A few pieces of red and crude black on white date from this period.

Pottery appears in greater abundance in the ruins of pre-Pueblo culture. Although the physical type of the inhabitants changes with the opening of the period, the cultural type is directly derived from that of the preceding period. The pottery types are genetically related to those of the post-Basket-Maker caves. The prevailing wares were black, black on white, and red. Cooking pots were made of black ware. The black on white bowls and ollas were elaborately but crudely decorated. The style is exclusively geometrical and angular, composed of patterns that may well have been influenced by textile technique. Important decorative motives were a stepped figure outlined with a number of parallel lines, and triangles similarly treated.

At the close of the pre-Pueblo period, we find a great increase of population and concentration in large communities. This great house period was the golden age of the Southwest, when the pueblo peoples reached their highest development in architecture and ceramics. None of these great houses were occupied for a long period. They were not strictly contemporaneous, neither did they follow one another, but there was considerable overlapping. Throughout the period there were great movements of population, first from the north southwards, followed by a withdrawal; the most southerly towns were abandoned and the population concentrated towards the center. It was these central sites that were occupied for the longest periods.

This period was marked by the emergence of a large number of highly differentiated types in architecture as well as in ceramics. In addition to the pottery types of the pre-Pueblo period a new type made its appearance, namely the characteristic corrugated ware. In this type the coiled technique was utilized for decorative purposes. These vessels were made of exceedingly fine coils and the corrugations were not smoothed out as in the painted types. The coils were further ornamented with regular flutings and patterns made by indentations in the soft clay. This ware reached the highest stage of technical excellence, and a good piece of coiled pottery is among the finest ceramic productions of the Southwest. This ware persisted for a very long period, and is found in greater or less quantities in all prehistoric pueblos. The forms of the vessels and the technique were fairly uniform over the whole Southwestern area and throughout the period.

Red ware was also made in varying quantities in all places; but the characteristic ware of the early pueblo period was the black-on-white. This was made at all early sites. The decorative types show marked diversity from place to place, but with a few notable exceptions the decoration is exclusively geometrical. An attempt to characterize the various types is beyond the scope of the present work. This black-on-white ware was succeeded in the later ruins by a variety of polychrome styles utilizing life forms in decoration, and in some places by decoration in glaze paint, the development and decay of which can be closely followed in a number of different sites. From all the late prehistoric ruins, pottery sequences can be obtained, either because these sites were occupied for longer periods, or because of the greater instability of ceramic art. The refuse heaps yield sherds of many different types, and by careful excavation these can be ranged in accurate chronological series. Data of this kind represent some of the most important material on the development of styles of art.

The polychrome styles of this late period show even greater local variation than the black on white. This is especially surprising in view of the very extensive migrations which occurred throughout this period, with the resultant opportunities for cultural interchange. Some of the sites which were occupied for brief periods only developed highly distinctive local types. Chihuahua, the Mimbres Valley and Casa Grande are three such sites, and their pottery is among the most strikingly individual ceramic products of the Southwest. The exquisite Mimbres Valley ware, for instance, is, in its treatment of animal forms, unique in the whole Southwest. It has no antecedents, no descendants, no cycle of development. It is a sport, appearing suddenly fully developed at the period of the greatest efflorescence of pueblo art, flourishing for a brief hour, and disappearing just as suddenly and leaving no traces behind. Is its brief and brilliant history bound up with the life of a single rarely gifted individual, the founder of a school of ceramic art? Kidder, among others, admits this possibility. The extent of the rubbish heaps and the unity of ceramic types show that the cities at which this and the equally distinctive Casa Grande ware were made were occupied for brief periods. These towns were abandoned. There is no sign of their having been destroyed, so it must be assumed that the inhabitants migrated to other towns, possibly northwards to the Little Colorado. But they did not take their art with them. They rather took over the ceramic style of the people among whom they settled. We look in vain for pottery of marked Lower Gila type at Zuni, although it is fairly well established that Zuni received accessions of population from that area. Each artistic type seems to be fairly closely connected with a particular geographical area, and does not seem to flourish outside of that area.

The Golden Age had already closed when the Spaniards first appeared in the Southwest. The population was declining and architecture and ceramics no longer showed the technical excellence of the early period. Glaze paint, which had been given up in favor of polychrome, was revived in several places, possibly under Spanish influence. The next 150 years were a period of gradual decline. In the years 1680-1700, the last great shift of population occurred. During the disturbance that followed the great rebellion of 1680 many towns were abandoned. It is probable that the population declined greatly in the years immediately preceding this. With the

year 1700 the archaeological record practically ends. Most of the villages occupied at that time are still inhabited and are therefore unavailable for systematic archaeological research. The investigations at Pecos, which was inhabited down to 1838, are bridging this gap. About 1850 the record recommences with the modern period.

Ceramic History of Zuni and Hopi Regions

With this very general outline in mind, we shall now turn to study in greater detail the archaeological records for the Zuni and Hopi districts. There is no archaeological material for Acoma.

The record is fullest for Zuni. Scattered through the Zuni valley, and within a short distance of the present town are some two hundred ruins, varying in size from single houses to villages of two hundred houses or more. None of these sites were inhabited for a long period, and it is more than probable that they were successively occupied. The pottery recovered from these sites shows so much overlapping in type that whatever may have been the general cultural history of the region, so far as ceramics are concerned, we are dealing with a single development. Of these sites at least six are historic towns although only Zuni is still inhabited. Those occupied at the time of the conquest were Hawikuh, Ketcipawa, Zuni (Halona),[2] Kyakima, Matsakya, Kwakina (probably) and an unidentified town referred to by Onate as "Aquinsa."

In 1916 Spier visited 167 of these sites and on the basis of a statistical examination of surface collections of potsherds tried to establish a chronology for the ruins of this area.[3] Using as his criterion the proportion of corrugated to other wares, he finds that the sites fall into two groups, that in which corrugated pottery is associated with red, black, buff and white wares, and that in which corrugated is associated with white only. The

[2] The Zunis refer to their town as Shiwinakwi, Halona and Itiwanna, but never as Zuni. Halona is used both for the present town and the prehistoric ruin on the south side of the river, where the trading store now stands. See Kroeber, 1917, p. 202, for the use of the name.

[3] Spier, 1917.

former group includes all the towns known to be historic, so the other group is assumed to be older.

At the beginning of his series is a ruin of slab-house type with all black-on-white pottery. At the end is contemporary Zuni which also makes only white ware with decoration in black and red paint. Between these two fixed points we have first a rise in the proportion of corrugated pottery, and a corresponding decline of black on white. This is followed by the period of red ascendancy. As red gains in importance, new techniques are introduced, first a polychrome red (i. e. black and white paint on red), then glaze replaces black paint and we have black glaze on red, and black glaze and white paint on red. Finally glaze replaces black paint on white. At this point he finds a gap in the record before we come to the historic villages. The scene shifts from the extreme west of the valley to the center, to sites with entirely different proportions of wares. Black assumes an important place, and buff decorated with brown paint and black glaze appears and advances rapidly. Red reappears but quickly vanishes; at a late period white increases rapidly, leading into the modern period. Because of the sudden appearance of buff as an important ware, Spier connects these later villages with the ruins to the west on the Little Colorado, rather than with the preceding period in the Zuni valley, and believes that the pottery sequences indicate extensive movements of population.

Unfortunately the sherds collected were not of sufficient size to make possible a detailed investigation of the types of decoration. Judging from the fragments illustrated in his paper, the decoration throughout the period was exclusively geometric, and, with the exception of a few sherds of the early black on white period, entirely angular. Dr. Spier is of the opinion that no important stylistic change occurred throughout the whole period, that even the substitution of glaze for flat paint had no appreciable effect on the types of design. However, he was not primarily interested in pottery as decorative art.

Although Dr. Spier's method and especial-

ly his premises are open to question, there can be no doubt that his outline of pottery sequences is, on the whole, correct.

During the years 1917-1923 Mr. F. W. Hodge made extensive excavations at Hawikuh, one of the historic Zuni towns which was occupied until 1680. In addition to uncovering the greater part of the ruins and recovering large amounts of pottery and other artifacts, a stratigraphic test was made in the plaza of the ancient town to determine the chronological sequence of pottery types. Unfortunately the complete report has not yet been published, but in a preliminary outline Hodge agrees, on the whole, with the findings of Spier.[4] He distinguishes nine separate types deposited in the following order:

I. Pre-Hawikuh. Black on white, black on red and corrugated. This type is found mostly in sherds and was never made at Hawikuh; it belongs rather to the period of the kivas near the town, which were already abandoned when Hawikuh was built.

II. Glaze 1. Two color glaze: red (orange) with black (greenish) glaze. Bowls with white exterior decoration. Geometric patterns.

III. Glaze 2. Two color glaze: white with black glaze. The exterior is sometimes left red and ornamented with white paint, or white paint and black glaze. Some life forms, especially stylized birds are found.

IV. Glaze 3. Three color glaze; white with black (green or maroon) glaze and red paint. Life forms are more common.

V. Polychrome 1. White (yellow) with black and red paint.

VI. Polychrome 2. Buff with decoration in orange, red, brown, black. Highly conventionalized animal figures.

VII. Polychrome 3. Ware heavier than VI, patterns and colors bolder.

VIII. Glaze 4. Green glaze used in conjunction with polychrome. Technically and artistically inferior to early glaze. Historic.

IX. Glaze 5. Black glaze on red; glaze crudely applied. Geometric patterns.

The last type was still on the ascendant when the record comes to a sudden stop with the abandonment of the pueblo, following the

[4] Hodge, 1924.

rebellion in 1680. The pottery of the last two periods is associated with objects of Spanish manufacture, and therefore probably represent the period of close contact with the Spaniards, that is, after the founding of the mission in 1629. It is probable that the advent of the Spaniards falls within the polychrome period.

Spier has excavated at a few points in Zuni pueblo. The quantity of pottery recovered is not sufficient for any detailed analysis, but it shows in the lower levels (5-16 feet) glazed and painted pottery that parallels the characteristic ware of the early historic villages. They appear at Zuni always as minor wares, but nevertheless furnish some clues as to what took place in the two centuries following the abandonment of Hawikuh. The sherds recovered are not of sufficient size to warrant any inferences in regard to the decorative motives employed, much less the general principles of design. Until more extensive diggings are made at Zuni this period from 1680-1850 must remain a blank. However, there is no doubt that the present Zuni types are not directly related to the Hawikuh wares. The last pottery made at Hawikuh was a degenerate glazed ware, showing badly controlled glaze on red ground. The patterns are exclusively geometric. Hodge considers this to be a recent imitation of his Type II, the earliest glaze ware made at Hawikuh. This conscious revival of an obsolete style is not without parallel in the Southwest, both in the present and the past.

The type of pottery with which the modern period opens is already familiar enough. It is entirely unlike anything which preceded it in the Zuni valley, and equally unlike anything outside except the contemporaneous Hopi pottery. Some few decorative motives, notably the scroll (Nos. 12, 13) are found in certain contemporary Rio Grande wares, especially San Ildefonso, but the handling of the decorative material and the very characteristic principles of design and composition are peculiar to Zuni. The modern style was already well developed in the very beginning of the past century. Dr. Kidder found in a late de-

posit at Pecos several sherds of Zuni pottery showing typical Zuni designs and technique. One sherd contained fragments of the design on the jar in Pl. III, a. There are a number of pots in the National Museum that are probably of equal age. A number of Zuni pots recovered by Dr. Kidder from Navaho graves in Cañon del Muerto belong to the same period. These finds all indicate a fairly well defined decorative style. The accompanying and preceding Pecos ware, which is typical for the whole Rio Grande region, shows nothing in any way related to the modern Zuni styles, and it is therefore fruitless to look for Zuni origins in that quarter. How and when this style arose is a problem whose solution must be sought in the rubbish heaps of Zuni. In the present state of our knowledge, there is no reason to believe that it had its origin outside of the Zuni valley.

A few very old pots in the Stevenson collection do not throw much light upon the origin of the present style.[5] These pieces do not belong to the present type, neither do they belong to the latest Hawikuh type. They resemble more closely than anything else certain old pieces in the Keam collection of Hopi pottery with which they are probably contemporaneous and to which they are undoubtedly related. This is by no means a "transitional" type in any sense but a chronological one. The fact that these jars survived to be included in the Stevenson collection made in 1879 would lead to the inference that they were made not much before 1850, possibly later. This would make them contemporaneous with pots of distinctly modern type, represented in one Pecos sherd and the Cañon del Muerto burials. We have thus evidence of a definite period in which the old style lingered on uncontaminated by a modern style which was already well established, and which was destined ultimately to displace it entirely.

We have already discussed at some length the changes that have taken place in the pottery of Zuni, within the brief modern period, but to complete this condensed history of the ceramic art of Zuni, we may repeat briefly

[5] See Pl. XX.

PLATE XX

ZUNI JARS, EARLY NINETEENTH CENTURY, USNM

[77]

what has taken place within the seventy-five years of intimate contact with white civilization.

The principal difference between the two periods is a greater variety of decorative motives and greater freedom of arrangement in the older style. Technically, the earlier pottery was no better in manipulation of material and application of design. The modern ware is, if anything, more accurately and tastefully painted. There has, however, been a decided decline in the liveliness of imgination as reflected in design. No new decorative motives or types of arrangement have been developed within the past fifty years to compensate for those which have been given up. We have already pointed out that this shrinkage may be due to the concentration of the craft in the hands of a few individuals. The younger generation of women are not interested in pottery, either as a household necessity or as an art. Whatever pottery is made at the pueblo is therefore the work of older women who all seem inclined to repeat those of their designs which have proved successful in the past.

The present sterility of Zuni art is a natural outcome of contact with white civilization and the general gradual disintegration of pueblo culture. It is a condition which we might expect to find in other places which have been exposed to the same influences. This, however, is by no means the case. At Acoma, San Ildefonso, and among the Hopi pottery has undergone radical changes within the past fifty years. New and beautiful types have come into existence under conditions analogous to those obtaining at Zuni. It is not easy to account for these differences.

To sum up: the history of Zuni pottery seems to fall into five main periods, as follows:

I. First painted period. Black on white; exclusively geometric decoration.

II. First period of glaze. Several types succeeding one another; decoration largely geometric.

III. Second painted period. Polychrome on yellow base; life forms prominent.

IV. Second glaze period. A brief revival of II (Historic).

V. Third painted period, modern. Black and red on white; geometric and life forms.

The Hopi record has been somewhat obscured owing to the fact that so much of the archaeological work in their district has been undertaken under the influence of an erroneous theoretical viewpoint, and before archaeological methods had reached their present development. Fewkes and other investigators of the late nineteenth century carried on their archaeological investigations under the influence of the clan migration legends that form so large a part of Hopi mythology, and endeavored to find in the various types of pottery found in different sites in the Hopi region the archaeological evidence of the truth of these traditions. In all these investigations they disregarded the chronological relationships between the various sites, and in this way entirely missed the essential point. Nevertheless, large quantities of pottery were recovered and made available for study. When the chronological relationships were once established by stratigraphic tests it was easy to arrive at an understanding of the ceramic history of this region.

As at other places, the two extremes of the series were fairly well fixed. At one end is the black on white ware whose great antiquity is nowhere disputed, and which has connections outside of the region; the other end of the series runs into modern times.

Kidder has established the chronological sequence of wares for the Hopi region by stratigraphic tests at two sites which were occupied for long periods, and by surface collections from a number of other places. The test sites were Old Shimopavi on Second Mesa, and Awatobi, an historic village on Antelope Mesa, and the seat of a Spanish mission.

I. The earliest ware from both of these sites is black on white, — the ware which at an early period was made all over the Southwest and which everywhere shows similar technical and artistic features. Found with this in the Hopi ruins is a small amount of orange ware with decorations in red and black (Kayenta polychrome) which is widely distributed in Northeastern Arizona. In both of these wares the decoration is entirely geometrical and largely angular.

II. Red with geometric decorations in black. This ware is similar to the earliest Hawikuh wares. The base color in later periods gradually fades out to orange and yellow, giving place slowly to

III. "Jeddito Yellow," a ware specialized in Tusayan, a clear yellow base with excellent decorations in brown. Angular geometric patterns predominate with, very rarely, representative forms. This ware takes its name from the numerous ruins in the Jeddito valley where it is found on the surface as the dominant ware. The transition is gradual into

IV. "Sikyatki." This ware, which takes its name from the ruin on First Mesa which has yielded the most varied and beautiful specimens, is characterized by a clear yellow surface with elaborate decorations in brown and red. The characteristic form is the shallow bowl, in the decoration of which highly conventionalized life forms predominate. This is a late pre-historic period, contemporaneous with the polychrome period of Hawikuh, with which it shares many characteristics of color, form, and the general treatment of animal forms. These two wares have either exerted a mutual influence on one another, or both have sprung from a common source. The Sikyatki is the more highly developed style.

The patterns which are used on Sikyatki pottery have been admirably illustrated in Fewkes' report on the site.[6] Unfortunately, however, the plates represent a high sampling of the ware. The specimens which are illustrated are not typical, but have been selected because of their intrinsic beauty and supposed symbolism. Nevertheless, it gives a fairly good idea of the style.

Water jars are rare, due perhaps to the fact that the collection is exclusively mortuary pottery. When they occur they are generally decorated with geometric ornaments in panelled bands. The small bowl is the characteristic shape, and is decorated on the inside with a single elaborately conventionalized bird or animal figure. The ruin of Sikyatki was abandoned when this style was at its height.[7]

It lingered on, however, at Awatobi, where it gradually declined into

V. "Mission." This ware, which is found on or near the surface at Awatobi, associated with articles of Spanish manufacture, is inferior to the preceding product of Sikyatki and Awatobi. The vessels are thick and heavy, the paste soft. The ground color is yellow or buff, with decorations in black and red, crudely executed. The beautiful and elaborate designs of the earlier designs have given way to simpler patterns with an increase of geometric forms. Material of this period is very slight in quantity. This was the predominant ware at Awatobi when the town was destroyed in 1700 by a war expedition from Walpi. It is found, however, in the rubbish heaps of Walpi, where it gradually gives way to

VI. Modern. This ware which flourished from 1850 to 1900 is well represented in our museums. It has a white or yellowish slip with decorations in black and red.

Collections include both water jars and bowls of various shapes and sizes. The water jars are globular with fairly small mouth and short necks. They do not, however, show the concave bases which are characteristic of Zuni and all the eastern pueblos. The jars are for the most part smaller than those of other places. Bowls, also are for the most part small and shallow, althought a few bowls with high straight rims are found. Most of the rims are incurved like the Sikyatki forms, or flaring. The decorations of the water jar is on the same general scheme as that of Zuni. For the small neck a simple border is used. The body is decorated from neck to base with widely spaced patterns, with a general horizontal effect. On some of the larger jars the characteristic Zuni layout of panels and bands is used. The most common, in fact, almost the only design is an eared scroll, the same motive as the common Zuni design. (No. 12.) Bowls are decorated on the interior, usually over the whole surface. In this position also the Zuni design (No. 12) is used, generally in pairs. With this a zigzag border (Zuni Nos.

---

[6] Fewkes, R. B. A. E. 17.

[7] Sikyatki is a two-period site, containing a large amount of Type III, Jeddito. This has found its way into the con- temporary ware, especially in the work of one potter who prefers the simple angular patterns of the older ware. See p. 55.

66-68) is employed. On bowls with flaring lips a panelled border of elaborately festooned scrolls is frequently used, the center of the bowl often being left undecorated. A common design for the exterior of bowl rims is Zuni design No. 59. The rule for its use, however, is not so fixed as at Zuni. The one exception to the universally geometric scheme of decoration is the frequent use of masked heads in the decoration of bowls. The most usual one of the impersonated gods to appear in pottery is the *Calako-mana*, a female deity associated with corn. She is also commonly represented on baskets. This representation of masked personages in household articles is, so far as I know, unique in pueblo art.[8]

This modern Hopi style is so very similar to the contemporary ware of Zuni that there is no doubt that there was some close historical connection. The various investigations of historic sites in the Rio Grande valley all show glazed wares dominant at the time of the general population shifts of 1680-1700. This would seem to conclusively rule out that the hypothesis that the modern style of pottery was the contribution of the Tewa settlers on First Mesa. The close resemblance to modern Zuni ware points rather in that direction.

The collection made over a number of years by Mr. Keam, and now in the Peabody Museum at Cambridge, comprises mostly pieces of this period. It also includes a large number of pieces which are unclassifiable and are apparently transitional between the modern and the early mission period. There is also some definitely archaeological material, mostly from Awatobi. The transitional pieces probably were heirlooms still in use in Hopi households in the years during which the collection was made. There are several such pieces in the Stevenson collection from Zuni and they still occasionally turn up. However it is dangerous to base any conclusions on such finds when the exact history of the particular piece is not known. Such precise in-

[8] Since the above was written Dr. Parsons has called my attention to two bowls so decorated which Hodge excavated from late deposits at Hawikuh.

formation is lacking for the Keam collection. More information is needed in regard to the period between 1700 and 1850. This is to be found in the rubbish heaps of Walpi.

In the first years of the present century the modern ware was suddenly displaced by

VII. Contemporary. This is a reversion to type IV, Sikyatki ware, the finest pottery of the Hopi region, and is the result of the efforts of one person.

In the year 1895 Dr. Fewkes carried on extensive excavations at Sikyatki, which is only three miles from the village of Hano, and is adjacent to the Hano peach orchards. Among Fewkes' workmen was a Hano man whose wife, Nampeyo, was one of the most expert potters of First Mesa. She frequently visited her husband at the excavations and showed the keenest interest in the pottery that was being uncovered. She was struck by the possibilities of the ancient designs and soon began imitating them on her own pottery. She had a great commercial success with the new ware, and the style was soon adopted by other women. How rapidly this process of displacement went on is a matter of conjecture. By 1924 when the writer was at First Mesa the displacement was complete. Although it is said that a few women still make the old ware, I was unable to find anyone making it, and I saw none of it at the store, whither the whole ceramic output of the Hopi women finds its way. One woman had in her possession a very fine red bowl of the old type which she treasured as an old family possession. She spoke of it as "very old, — maybe ten or twelve years. It is the kind the old people used to make. They do not make them like this any more." A number of bowls of this kind are still in use in the more conservative villages of Second Mesa, where native products have given way to imported articles more slowly. These bowls were all made on First Mesa. With these exceptions the new style of pottery has entirely displaced the old in household use, as well as commercially. Bowls which are used especially for semi-ceremonial meals are all of the same type as find their way to the store. A particular form of large globular storage jar which is made only for household use and only in rare instances becomes an article of commerce, is always made of yellow clay, with decorations in the Sikyatki manner. It would seem, therefore, that although the motives underlying the recent revolution in decorative style were largely commercial, esthetic preference played some part in the rapid assimilation of the new style.

One of the most important phenomena in this change of style is the fact that the Sityatki type was taken over entirely. The new ware is not a blending of Sikyatki and modern types, but is rather a return to the Sikyatki style. The prehistoric shapes were adopted along with the designs. Even the composition of the ware changed and a soft yellow paste, similar but inferior to the Sikyatki ware displaced the white slip of the nineteenth century pottery. It is probable that the two styles existed side by side for some years, some women preferring one type, some the other, but no hybridization resulted from the contact of the two styles. The thoroughness of the assimilation of the new style has already been noticed, some potters even dreaming "original" designs of Sikyatki inspiration.

At the risk of being repetitious, I have described in some detail the Hopi sequence of pottery types, because it is one of the few places where we can see a decorative style changing under our eyes, and because the change has been so complete and compressed into so brief a period. The whole Hopi sequence can be summarized as follows:

I. Black on white period. Entirely geometric ornament.

II. Late prehistoric period. A gradual development of colored wares and animal ornament, reaching its highest development at Sikyatki village.

III. Historic period. A gradual return to white wares and geometric ornament.

IV. Contemporary. A recent revival of II.

We have already noted with regret the absence of any archaeological material from Acoma. A very small collection of sherds from Acoma rubbish heaps shows affiliations with the Rio Grande, rather than with the west. The material is so fragmentary that it is merely an indication. But whatever the early history of Acoma pottery may be, it has undergone since the middle of the nineteenth century changes no less striking in their way than those which have taken place at Walpi, and which apparently occurred without the particular commercial stimulus which gave rise to the changes on First Mesa.

We have described (p. 36) the outstanding characteristics of Acoma art of the 70's, but it may not be amiss to recapitulate here. The general scheme of decoration was simple, usually a single broad irregular band of design about the center of the jar. It is perhaps misleading to refer to this decoration as a band; it is not a band in the sense of being confined within parallel bands, but I use the term rather to indicate that the patterns follow one another in horizontal sequence with white background showing above and below. The preferred arrangement was in alternating units, closely interlocked. Sometimes the pattern fills almost completely the whole decorative field, but at no time is there an elimination of background such as characterizes the present ware. The background is always present, sometimes in small quantities, it is true, but it is always very obviously background. The pattern never crowds the background out of the picture and becomes itself a background for something else. The older patterns are bold in line and striking in their use of color, but nevertheless the older generation of potters were not colorists in the same sense as the present generation. There is not the use of color for its own sake and the subtle balancing of tones. As elsewhere in the pueblo region, color is here subordinated to line and form. The decorative motives themselves are mostly of a very different character, but a few of the present motives appear in the older jars, for instance, the checkerboard and some of the oval leaf or petal-like forms. Plates XI and XIV show the chasm that separates the two styles.

The new style was already established in

the early years of the twentieth century, for we have several specimens collected in those years. There is no collection of pottery made during the intervening years, so exactly what happened between 1879 and 1905 is a matter of conjecture. The two types are so utterly different in their whole approach to the decorative problem that although there are some few points of contact, it seems exceedingly unlikely that the one style developed gradually into the other. The collections made early in the twentieth century show no transitional pieces, although there is some overlapping of the two types.

Somewhat similar and no less striking is the history of ceramic art at San Ildefonso, where also a radical change in decorative style has taken place within the present generation. Within the modern period, that is, the period for which we have definitely datable material, roughly since the middle of the last century, we find the following sequence of forms. During the last half of the nineteenth century a type of polychrome ware was made which was closely related to other Rio Grande types. Water jars were given a yellowish white slip above and a bright orange-red slip below. The white portion was decorated with widely spaced, lightly executed patterns in black paint. The designs were similar in general style to other Rio Grande wares, but were more elaborate and highly integrated. The spiral was a conspicuous decorative motive. A red ware decorated in black was also made, but was exceedingly rare. Towards the end of the century the pottery of this pueblo declined steadily, until by 1907 the degeneration was complete. At that time the pottery of San Ildefonso was in as bad a way as is that of Santo Domingo and Laguna today. In the year 1907 the pottery recovered from excavations on the Pajarito Plateau aroused the interest of the San Ildefonso workmen and their wives and resulted in a renaissance of ceramic art in the village. In this case the prehistoric types were not copied, but the types of the nineteenth century were revived and developed with certain changes such as the introduction of red paint

into the black designs. Atrocities of American inspiration were abandoned in favor of the traditional ware of the village. Here, too, the reawakened interest in ceramics was quickly rewarded with commercial success, and as a result the ware continued to improve in technical and artistic excellence. The leaders of this movement were Maria Martinez and more especially her husband, Julian, who decorated all of Maria's pottery. He is a skillful painter, and a man of considerable originality and sensitiveness to problems of design. He worked for some years at the Santa Fé Museum and at various archaeological diggings, and had opportunity to study large quantities of pottery from various sources. He was a discriminating student and a receptive one, and he adapted and introduced into his village a large number of designs derived from various archaeological sources. He favored especially Hopi (Sikyatki) designs. New forms were also introduced, including a shallow bowl decorated only on the outer rim. The whole type of pottery was undergoing a gradual transition, when in 1921 a new element was introduced. Polished black pottery had always been made in small quantities at San Ildefonso, although it never reached the importance it attained at the neighboring pueblo of Santa Clara. However, in 1921, Maria Martinez invented a process of applying designs in dull black paint to the polished surface immediately before firing, so that in the finished product the design appears as if in intaglio on the polished black background. This ware was exhibited that year at the Santa Fé fair where it took first prize, and, more important, found immediate favor with the traders and curio buying public, among whom it commanded hitherto unheard-of prices. As a result of this phenomenal success the ware was soon imitated by other potters, and has now become the dominant ware of the pueblo, displacing the older polychrome and black and red types. In 1924 the same process was applied to the polished red pottery, and the resulting product bids fair to rival the black in popularity. The other painted wares have practically disappeared.

When the writer visited the pueblo in 1925 only the polished black and polished red were being made, although a few pieces of polychrome were offered for sale. This change in the type of ware has not been without its far-reaching effect on design. The style depends for its decorative effect on the balancing of masses. The older types of decoration do not lend themselves at all to this kind of treatment, and have been given up in favor of a far simpler style. Plates XIX and XXXV-XXXVIII illustrate the extent of this change.

A similar revival is just beginning at Santo Domingo. The ceramic product of this village has reached a lamentable state of decay. The atrocities which are turned out there by the hundreds equal the worst products of San Ildefonso at its lowest ebb. Mr. Kenneth Chapman, who fostered the revival of San Ildefonso is doing a similar good work at Santo Domingo. He has induced Monica Silva, a Santa Clara woman married at Santo Domingo, to make for him a complete collection of old Santo Domingo designs, drawn largely from pottery in various collections in Santa Fé. The original drawings are in the New Mexico Historical Museum, but Monica has a set of photographic reproductions which she consults in her work. She and another woman are now making jars according to the best Santo Domingo tradition. Stimulated by the success of San Ildefonso potters with their decorated black ware, Monica has begun to make this also, using however the classical Santo Domingo designs. These traditional patterns being essentially a treatment of surfaces in two colors are especially adapted to this new ware. It will be interesting to watch the development of this style, and see whether it will supersede the black and white here also.

It is important to follow all these contemporary currents in pueblo art, and a thorough investigation of just what is going on in each place will throw considerable light on the general problem of esthetic development. Nevertheless, undue importance should not be given to them. The movements have been too commercial and too largely the results of outside influences. Certainly at San Ildefonso and Santo Domingo the artistic development has been inspired and fostered by outside influences. Among the Hopi, although the motive for the change in decorative style is more commercial than esthetic, the movement is wholly native. There is no doubt that it was Nampeyo and not the traders and ethnologists who was responsible for the revival of the Sikyatki style. Its rapid adoption by other potters was, of course, due to its commercial success, but the complete assimilation and subsequent efflorescence of the style point to something more than commercial expediency in its adoption.

At Acoma, however, we have the phenomenon of a complete change in style, which seems due to nothing more than a change of taste. I cannot see any commercial motive behind this change. However, the date and exact circumstance of the change are still unknown. If some old potter can still be found who remembers making the older style, any information she could give would be of greatest value.

Relative Stability of Technique and Style

As we trace the history of ceramic types over long periods of time, and compare modern products of different villages, one of the most striking conditions is the variety of decorative styles which have grown up upon the basis of similar or even identical techniques. Even at San Ildefonso the actual technical processes employed in the production of polished black ware are not so different from those used in the manufacture of polychrome as the difference in the appearance of the ware would indicate. The composition of the paste, the methods of molding, rough finishing and firing, are the same for all pueblos. These, after all, are the basic processes of ceramic technique; all else is ornament. There is nothing in the surface finish of a vessel that adds in any way to its utilitarian value. But even techniques of ornamentation are parallel. In all polychrome wares, the use of slips, the ways in which they are applied, the use of the polishing stone to obtain a smooth surface, the implements for applying pigments and the ways in which they are handled, and indeed the pigments themselves, show striking similarities. Archaeological material indicates that these methods have been constant over a very long period of time. Early ruins yield both coiled and slipped pottery, unmistakable evidence of the antiquity of the present methods of manipulating the material. There have been recovered also many of the tools of pottery making: scrapers, polishing stones, mortars for the mixing of pigments; indicating that technical processes were developed to their present state at a comparatively early time, and have ever since formed a fairly constant background for fluctuations in decorative style. It has frequently been claimed that technology is the domain of cultural activity most subject to change. Styles of art are, apparently, even more unstable. They have all the usually accepted indices of hoary antiquity, — they are "traditional," they are developed and passed on by non-rational mental processes, they frequently have apparently profound religious and social associations, all conditions which contribute to extreme stability according to the theories of many social psychologists. It is, therefore, in some ways rather unexpected to find that art is one of the most evanscent of human activities, one that is highly susceptible to individual mutation.

Relative Stability of Religious and Secular Art

We have referred in several places to certain ceremonial objects made of clay. Of these the most important are sacred meal bowls and drums. The drums are large globular jars over the mouth of which is stretched a hide. They are the primitive equivalent of the tympani of the modern orchestra. These drums are ordinarily made of reddish clay undecorated. At Zuni, however, painted drums are sometimes made. They are slipped in white like household pottery, and painted with figures of animals. Two of these drums are shown in Pl. IX, p. 26. The decorations

obviously have nothing whatever in common with those of household pottery. The figures used are different, but more fundamental are the crudeness of technique and totally different handling of the decorative field. These drums are used exclusively by medicine cults. The paintings on them are of the same character as those on the walls of certain rooms in which these cults hold their esoteric ceremonies. They belong to the whole complex of religious paraphernalia: house paintings, sand-paintings, altar boards, masks, etc. They are not, strictly speaking, pottery at all. It is a purely fortuitous circumstance that they are made of clay. One of the designs used on these drums has recently slipped over into the decoration of household vessels. This is the famous deer pattern, so unique in pueblo art, whose presence has been attributed by some archaeologists to Spanish influence. If its derivation is Spanish, it is at least two steps removed from its origin. The interesting thing, however, is that on household vessels, it is so differently treated from on ceremonial objects. It is incorporated into the decorative scheme by surrounding it always with a graceful arch. In the series of Zuni designs drawn for me, the deer as such is never isolated as a design. I have seen no painted drums from other pueblos and do not know if they exist. However, I have seen drawings of house paintings in other pueblos, especially Acoma and Jemez, all strikingly like the Zuni paintings. This type of ornament, if it can be considered such, has, therefore, a fairly wide distribution at the present time, although its use on clay drums seems confined to Zuni.

What has been said of drums applies, though in a less degree, to meal bowls also. These also are decorated without regard to the rules of style which govern the ornamentation of household objects. As on drums, the designs on meal bowls are crudely naturalistic, the prevailing subjects, in addition to cloud symbols, being serpents, frogs, tadpoles, and dragon flies, — animals all associated with springs in mythology and folk belief. These, too, are all familiar symbols on other types of ceremonial objects, especially masks. Although there is some attempt at formal arrangement in the placing of these symbols on the bowl, the meal bowl is as definitely outside the ceramic complex as the drum. Both in symbolism and general style of decoration the Zuni meal bowl lies closer to similar objects of San Ildefonso than to the household ware from Zuni. The ceremonial objects of San Ildefonso also have nothing in common with the ceramic art of that pueblo. Meal bowls from Cochiti and First Mesa belong to the same general type. The Zuni meal bowls in Pl. VIII are all from the Stevenson collection of 1879. The square type is no longer made here, but it is common in the east. I did not see modern meal bowls being made in any of the eastern pueblos, but that is probably because no objects of ceremonial character would be shown to strangers in these villages. However, women showed me square and round vessels, which, although made for sale, were said to be derived from the traditional meal bowl. All had modelled rims, and were decorated with symbolic designs applied without regard to the principles of design prevailing in the decoration of other pottery. Most prominent among these designs was the cloud symbol which appears with slight modifications in petroglyphs, meal paintings, mask designs, altar paintings, dance kilt embroideries, and many other ceremonial objects, all the way from the Rio Grande to Oraibi. An exhaustive study of mask designs shows that these too are widely distributed among the different pueblos. The stabilizing influence in these mask paintings is not tradition. New masks are invented constantly, and there is nothing in the religious sentiments of the group that would tend to restrict these new masks to traditional types. The psychological basis for the stability of religious ornament is quite different. Its purpose is magical, not esthetic. Symbols which have proved effective are used on appropriate objects. Since the primary motivation is not esthetic, there is no tendency to play with the design or use it as a means for individual expression. In so far as the design is used mechanistically to produce a desired effect in the environment, it is in itself a technique of control. There is little tendency among primitive people to improve upon a satisfactory technique. It is from this angle that we must approach the problem of the relation between fixed symbolism — as different from mere interpretation in religious terms — and stability in design.

VII

CONCLUSION

The tendency for the artistic productions of all peoples to become fixed in definite forms characteristic of particular groups and particular periods led us at the beginning of our investigation to ask two questions: What, among naive people, are the factors conditioning the form of response of the individual to the esthetic impulse, and what influences in turn produce changes in these conditioning factors? It was our hope that an intensive study of the processes of artistic creation among a primitive people would in some measure illuminate this problem in the dynamics of culture.

The limitation of the field of inquiry to the manufacture of pottery by the Pueblo Indians was dictated largely by practical considerations. Here we have an art still practised in certain villages under aboriginal conditions. This art has a long history which, due to the indestructible nature of the material and the zeal of archaeologists, is known to us in great detail. Furthermore, the plastic arts yield most readily to analysis; in them it is comparatively easy to isolate purely formal elements.

The creation of beautiful form in clay is subject from the start to two kinds of limitations — those imposed by the nature of the material and by the purpose of the object. From the point of view of art, clay is one of the most versatile of all materials. Endless variation is possible in form, finish and color. Ornament may be evolved from the plastic nature of the material or applied in colored pigments. Most of the common ceramic techniques have been known and practised in the area studied. Some of them had already been tried and abandoned in prehistoric times.

The second set of limitations, those imposed by utilitarian considerations, seems less obvious. However, the clay vessel of the Southwest is always an article that serves two functions. It is primarily an utensil — in this case a container for water or food.[1] It is also an object whose form gives pleasure directly to the maker and user. Among the people who provided the basis of this study, and, indeed, among primitive people in general, it is the utilitarian aspect of objects and activities that holds the center of interest. With few exceptions the creation of objects solely for their own beauty is confined to the most highly sophisticated groups. It is doubtful if in our own society the practise of the arts is ever without secondary motivation — display, for instance, or compensation. Despite the preoccupation of our primitive potters with the utilitarian aspect of their product, they are fully aware of its esthetic significance. "Pretty, but not strong," is a comment that is often heard and which evaluates the object in terms of its two functions.

Within the limits set by these external factors great variability is still possible. All the people who came within the scope of the investigation recognized the desirability of using interest in form as a means of personal expression and gratification. Yet everywhere we have the mysterious phenomenon of style limiting still further the artists' freedom of expression. On the basis of identical technical processes each village has developed an easily recognizable type of pottery, distinctive in form, texture and ornament. Within each group the product shows surprising uni-

[1] A single figurine of clay, probably of religious significance has been recovered from an early ruin. Except for this, pottery is a household art.

formity in technical and esthetic characteristics.

Of the principles of design which produce these characteristic forms the makers are, with but few exceptions, entirely unconscious. Their unconscious sensitivity to form is especially marked in the modelling of vessels. With no more definite guide than their perception of form, they reproduce accurately and without hesitation the characteristic vessel of their group, and this notwithstanding that the technical limitations are such that the finished form must be clearly foreseen at an early stage. After the walls are half built, no corrections are possible.

Except at Zuni, where designs are consciously built up of recognized elements, artists are equally unconscious of the principles governing the structure of their ornamental designs. These too, are sensed intuitively. Everything, including the terminology of design, leads to the conclusion that decorative style is the product of unconscious and non-rational mental processes. Frequently the acceptance of the prevailing style is in distinct contradiction to the artist's conscious and expressed intent.

Since the artist is largely unaware of the processes determining the character of her designs, her conscious preoccupation is chiefly with matters of technical perfection. Soundness of structure, regularity of form, perfection of finish, delicacy and regularity of ornament are the features stressed in criticism and, even more markedly, in instruction. A girl receiving instruction in pottery making is told, "Paint anything you like, only put it on straight."

Nor is it likely that the potter is influenced in the least by the significance of her designs. The use of symbols is confined to pottery designed for ceremonial use. Although there is a marked tendency to associate designs with important facts of daily life, the association is so tenuous and so variable that it must be regarded as a secondary process. The finished design suggests an object or a situation, and is named accordingly. The same name is applied to designs having no objective resemblance; the same design is differently named by different individuals, and by the same individual at different times.

The emphasis on originality and individualism in design is general in all villages and among all potters. It indicates that everywhere art is regarded as a technique of individual expression. Theoretically there are no limitations upon the whim of the artist. We may conclude that the uniformity of style in any group is not due either to conscious desire on the part of the artists, or to pressure from without. The artist makes no conscious bid for public approbation. She paints to please only herself, although she is obviously influenced by current taste. However, conformity is no means of achieving approbation; the palm is awarded for originality. Since this is so, why do we so often encounter stereotypes, and, to question more profoundly, why do we have styles at all?

Style undoubtedly arises in the dependence of artists upon the visual image, either consciously called forth, dreamed or otherwise involuntarily evoked. Some few potters even supplement this subjective process by recourse to pattern books of one sort or another. These visual images, among the vast majority of people, are of things once directly perceived. Often, as in dreams, they are composites of different experiences, the familiar elements appearing in new combinations. It is precisely this sort of modified reproduction that characterizes some of the best examples of primitive art.

Stereotypes are due, unfortunately, to human mediocrity — in this case the absence of the creative faculty among many excellent craftsman. This is natural — natural in a dire sense. Compared with other natural phenomena, human behavior is ephemeral as the clouds of heaven. The human mind is a marvel of inventiveness compared to the force that reproduces species unchanged through countless thousands of generations. In view of this overwhelming stability in natural forms, it is not surprising that the creative spark is only rarely vouchsafed. The creative genius in human affairs is analagous to the biological sport that effects a mutation of species.

However, at infrequent intervals a person thus gifted does appear to bless humanity. One of the qualities of genius is the ability to experience mentally what has not been experienced sensually, and to embody this unique experience in tangible form. When such a person functions in the field of art, he may produce those sudden mutations in style that mark the history of the arts among all peoples.

Among the people studied there have been two such revolutions in recent years, and in each case the revolution in style can be traced to a striking personality. Nampeyo, a potter of Hano, revived and adapted the ancient ware of Sikyatki. Undoubtedly the original stimulus came from outside, but it was Nampeyo's unerring discrimination and lively perception that vitalized what would otherwise have been so much dead wood. She did not copy Sikyatki patterns, her imagination recreated the Sikyatki sense of form.

An even more striking personality is Julian Martinez of San Ildefonso. His wife, Maria, who takes the credit for the work of the family, is an excellent craftsman. Together they invented a new technical process and Julian, who had previously decorated much of her pottery, developed a new style of ornament suitable to the new ware. Material in the form of decorative motives he took wherever he found it. His discriminating and imaginative use of what came his way has produced a style of rare distinction.

In both these cases the new style has within a few years completely displaced old types of ware and ornament. During the brief period that the two styles existed side by side, there was no hybridization or mutual contamination.

In two cases mutation has been the result of an outside influence — the encouragement of white people interested in reviving aboriginal arts — working upon an individual endowed with technical equipment and creative imagination. Every group is constantly subjected to outside influences, but unless there

is something there, the stimulus does not take. No amount of white encouragement has been able to effect a revival of ceramics at Zuni. The same people who have had such success at San Ildefonso have used the same tactics at Zuni, and quite without result. Only the same old stereotypes are produced. It would seem that there is no one at Zuni whose imagination can be fired by offers of prizes or pictures of beautiful pottery.

The history of ceramic art in the Southwest has been, in general, a process of diversification from a common basis, with increasing variety and instability in the later periods — the periods characterized by great movements of populations. Everywhere there have been two historic processes at work, gradual development in the same general direction, punctuated by sudden mutations, sometimes revivals, followed by the displacement of the old type by the new. This phenomenon may be the direct result of purely external forces, such as conquest or colonization, but then again, there may be internal forces at work. Certainly there is no evidence to justify the assumption that artistic developments are regularly the results of definite movements of population. Our own analysis of changes in recent years seem to indicate that sudden changes in decorative style are rather the result of general cultural instability working upon the mind of a sensitive individual.

The writer has studied other artistic productions of the Zuni and other pueblo tribes, especially their tales, songs, chants, dances and rituals. The analysis of these forms must be deferred to some other place. However all of them are the response to a double motivation — the achievement of some obvious external end, — frequently the control of supernatural forces, — and the gratification of the esthetic sense.

Among the most spectacular and important Zuni rituals are large group dances by masked impersonators. The beings impersonated are rain gods, and the impersonation is a magical technique for producing rain by compelling the presence of the divinity. The compulsive power lies in the mask. The dance is a highly complex form, combining song, movement and pictorial elaboration. These external features are varied in accordance with general principles of style that are not essentially dissimilar to those of decorative art. There is a great premium on originality in songs, and good song makers are held in great honor. All this seems to be a conscious artistic elaboration of a ceremony whose primary character depends upon the fetishistic power of the mask.

The mask itself is made of leather freshly painted and adorned with feathers each time it is used. It is painted with highly conventional representations of faces. The treatment of the features and the arrangement of secondary patterns are in accordance with certain purely formal principles. In fact, the mask itself is a work of art, and is so regarded by the Zuni. In describing to me one of the most sacred masked ceremonies, the initiation of boys into the mysteries of the masked god cult, a Zuni remarked, "The children do not mind being whipped by the Salimopia. They are such pretty dancers."

Songs, prayers, rituals, all have their purely formal characters, often greatly elaborated. Indeed there seems to be no field of human behavior which may not be subjected to formal elaboration. It is a characteristic of all linguistic development; social grouping, economic arrangements frequently have their distinctly esthetic character. We are working towards a definition of art. It is the elaboration of the formal elements of objects and activities for their own sake. By this means civilizations achieve style.

APPENDIX I

ZUNI DESIGNS

APPENDIX I

ZUNI DESIGNS

No.	Use	Names and Meaning [1]	
		1924	1925
1	Prayer-meal bowl.	Dragon flies (*Cúmaikolowe*). Used in this form on sacred meal bowl.	Two dragon flies calling the rain (*Cúmaikolowe atci ḷitopa*).
2	Prayer-meal bowl.	*Kólowisi.*	*Kólowisi.*
3	Body of water-jar (This design is used on the ancient jar in which the Priest of the South keeps his sacred bundle.)		Clouds with eyes (*aweḷuya tunapa*) and feathers with eyes (*labanane tunapa*).
4	Body of water-jar.	Cloud stripe (*aweḷuya wapanapa*) A prayer for rain.	a. Cloud stripe (*aweḷuya ťsipopa*). Striped bead. b. *Ocokwinne ťsipopa.* c. Red triangle (*nitepowa cilowa*).
5	Body of water-jar.	a. Black steps (*hewi'etcik'winne*). b. Straight steps (*hemowisiwe*). c. Neck stripe (*witcitsipopa*). Black steps for the black clouds, straight steps for the rain people to come down.	(a) and (b) clouds joined together (*aweḷuya iyulipa*). c. Red neck triangle (*witci nitepowa cilowa*).
6	Body of water-jar.	Striped circle (*ťsipo bitsulia*). The clouds make a circle therefore there will not be any rain.	Cloud circle (*aweḷuya bitsulia*).
7	Body of water-jar.	Clouds struggling (*aweḷuya iťsumenawe*).	Striped steps (*hewi'etci ťsipopa*).
8	Body of water-jar.	Heart stripes (*ikyena ťsipopa*).	Square within heart (*maiya k'okci etton ikyena*).
9	Body of water-jar (with 10 or 11) or center of bowl.	*hepakinne* "sunflower."	*hepakinne* (painting on Salimopiya mask).

[1] Many of the designs were finished only after the writer left Zuni in 1924, and the names and interpretations of these designs were recorded by Dr. Ruth F. Benedict.

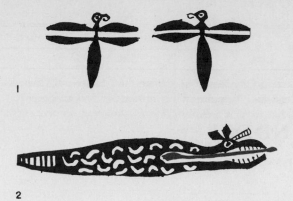

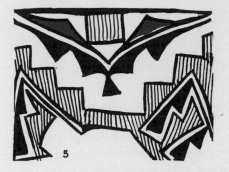

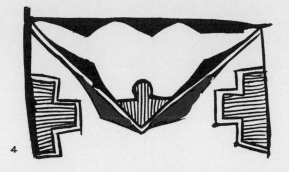

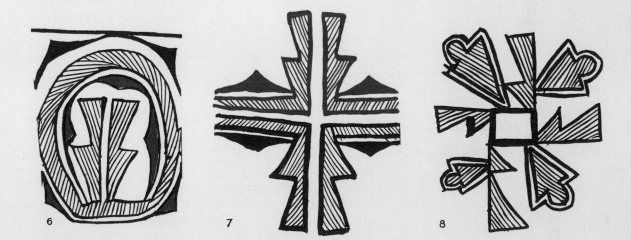

PLATE XXI

ZUNI DESIGN ELEMENTS

1, 2, for prayer-meal bowls; 3, on ancient ceremonial jar; 4-8, for bodies of jars

No.	Use	Names and Meaning	
		1924	1925
10	Body of water-jar (usually with No. 9) used also in interior of bowls).	Deer in house of flowers. Because the ground is painted black, not red, it is a prayer for damp earth. The women want soft ground to plant their gardens.	Deer in house of flowers (*na'lan k'yakwen'uteapa*). He is standing on the earth.
11	Body of water-jar or interior of bowls; on jar used with No. 9 or No. 16.	The deer's house (*nawe aw-an k'yakwenne*). We paint the deer so that our husbands may have good luck in hunting. Deerskins are so expensive we cannot buy them any more, and so we like to have pictures of the deer in our houses like the white people have pictures of God.	Deer house (*na'lan k'yakwen-ne*).
12 13	Body of water-jars; 4 or 8 arranged between vertical panels; also used in bowls, generally in threes.	Crook (*netsikânne*). This represents the drumstick used by fraternities (*tatsikânne*) in their ceremonies. It is made of willow turned back on itself and tied.	Large crook (*netsikâ łanne*). A prayer in rain. The crook belongs to the societies and they pray for rain, too. (a) Feathers (*lapanawe*). (b) Crook (*netsikânne*).
14	Body of water-jar.	Cirrus clouds (*pi'tcinawe su-łayawe*).	Milky way with crooks (*upi-yalan netsipopa*).
15	Body of water-jar.		Baby crooks (*wihetsanna net-sikâwe*) with triangles along the edge (*nitep'owa anpatło-pa*).
16	Body of water-jars in vertical panel in combination with 10, 11, 12, 13.	Grandfather standing (*nanna elaye*). A prayer for long life.	Crook circle (*netsikâ p'itsu-lia*).
17	Body of jar, same as No. 19.	Little cloud torn by the wind (*awełuyan tsanna it'siatikia*). Because he did not go to dances the little cloud was torn in two by the west wind.	Striped clouds with Milky Way (*awełuya kucoktanne*).
18	Body of jar.	Lying cloud. "A person who is not straight in life will not be straight when he comes to be a cloud."	Lightning checks (*wilonanne kucoktaya*). This stops the lightning so that there will not be any rain.
19	Body of jar, in vertical panel.	Little cloud (*awełuyan tsan-na*). The little cloud left all alone in the sky after a storm.	Clouds meet together with Milky Way (*awełuyan iyan-iktocnapa kucoktaya*).

9

10

11

12

13

14

15

PLATE XXII
Zuni design elements
9-15, for bodies of jars

[95]

No.	Use	Names and Meaning	
		1924	1925
		She is left alone when the other rain-makers come to make rain because during her life she never went to dances. She is lonely and the Milky Way comes to visit her. Cf. No. 46.	
20	Body of jar, in narrow horizontal band, with No. 10, etc.	Water birds (*wotsanawe*). "We like to paint the water-birds because they live in the water and so the jar will never be empty."	Two birds (*wotsana'atci*). They have crooks on their tails.
21	Body of jar used in narrow horizontal band with No. 10, etc.	Crooks joined together (*netsikâ iyulipa*).	Crooks joined together (*netsikâ'iyulipa*). These are the black clouds and the red clouds coming together.
22	Body of jar.	Crooks joined together with feathers (*netsikâ iyulipa lacowapa*). A prayer for beautiful music. We use the drumsticks a great deal because they are valuable. They make a sound we like to hear.	Crooks with feathers joined together (*netsikâ lacow'iyulipa*). This is for the katchinas. They have eyes like this and they wear feathers.
23	Body of jar.	Crooks meeting face to face (*netsikâ 'iyaniktocnapa*). These are the crooks (*telnawe*) of the rain priests, therefore they are a prayer for rain.	Crooks with feathers (*netsikâ lacowapa*). "These are like the feathers hanging from the masks of katcinas. Some of the katcinas have designs painted on the back of the masks, with feathers hanging from them.
24	Body of jar.	Prayer bow (*t'ewusu pi'lanne*). A prayer, like meeting for prayer.	Red triangle with eyes (*wopuliwe cilowa nitepowa tunapa*).
25	Body of jar.	Bow with horns and feathers (*pi'ta saiapa lacowapa*). Some of the katcinas in the mixed dance carry bows to frighten people. There is an eye at each end to show that it is made into a person.	Jar stomach design (*te'l an tsulakya t'sinanne*).
26	Body of jar.	Crossed steps (*itapotci hewietciwe*).	a. Black steps (*hewi'etciwe kwinne*). b. Square (*maiyak'okcipa*).

PLATE XXIII

Zuni design elements

16-23, for bodies of jars

[97]

No.	Use	Names and Meaning	
		1924	1925
			The black clouds and the real clouds are coming together. The black clouds are snow clouds and before they come together the red clouds come between them so that they will not meet and make snow.
27	Body of jar.	Clouds quarreling with the rainbow (*lowe amitolan ani-p'eyenawe*). The rainbow stops the red clouds, but we shall have rain anyway, because the other clouds come above the rainbow. A prayer for rain triumphing over unfavorable conditions.	Striped steps with Milky Way (*hewi'etciwe t'sipopa*) (*kucokta*).
28	Body of jar.	All clouds meet together in Itiwana (*temła 'iłonakia*). A prayer in dry weather.	Striped jar design (*te'lan icinan t'sipopa*).
29	Body of jar.		Feathers and downy feathers in one place (*lacowapa lapanapa wopulia*). The clouds should come right here to this place.
30	Body of jar.	Snow clouds and thin clouds. A prayer for snow rather than rain.	Wavy striped clouds. (*aweluya welonawa t'sipopa*).
31	Body of jar.	Damp spring with snow blanket, rain blanket and falling rain. A prayer for rain and snow.	Hanging feathers (*welo'labanapa*). The feathers call the rain when they hang.
32	Body of jar.	Checked ear (*lacoktin kucoktapa*). This is the design painted on the mask of Wooden Ears, one of the katcina.	Wavy square with downy feathers (*maiyak'okci weloatinane lacowapa*).
33	Body of jar below neck.		Striped triangles hanging down (*nitebowa t'sipanilenapa*). This is like rain falling far off. It looks like stripes in the sky.
34	Body of jar below neck.		Striped arrow point with triangle outside (*kiatowa t'sipopa, nitep'owa anpaltopa*).

24

25

26

27

28

29

30

31

PLATE XXIV
ZUNI DESIGN ELEMENTS
24-31, for bodies of jars

[99]

No.	Use	Names and Meaning	
		1924	1925
35	Body of jar.	Star makes the road light (*moweatcunona t'ekohanana-we*). A prayer of women that the stars may make the darkness light and make the road straight for husbands out at night.	Wavy checks (*kucokta welon-apa*). This is for the Milky Way to keep the sky bright at night.
36	Body of jar. Neck of jar or inside of bowl.	Dragon fly (*cumaikoli*). He has been caught in the rain and the wings stand out straight and bedraggled. A prayer for rain.	Butterfly calling the rain.
37	Inside of bowl.	Spider web. (*lotsito an uhe-pilanne*). We always want to see the spider in her web so that we may learn to weave well. "Did you touch the spider's web?" is what we say when we see a beautiful piece of weaving. A prayer for proficiency in weaving.	a. Feathers (*lawe*). b. Crooks (*netsikâwe*). c. Yucca suds (*kukwiwe*). This last is the same as the packet of seeds that all the Masked Gods carry and which represents their heart. These are all things the Masked Gods wear.
38	Center of bowl.	Flowers everywhere except at Itiwana (*uteawe ulanaye itiwa sakayaye*). The flowers are all around the middle. A woman at Hecokta prays for rain on her fields.	Red crooks and star (*netsikâ cilowa moweatcunne*).
39	Center of bowl.	Rain blanket (*litokia pa'in-ne*). A prayer for rain.	Crooks joined together inside the bowl (*netsika'iyulina salan etton*). This is a design used by Masked Gods on the top of the head. It represents many rain clouds coming together quickly from all directions.
40	Center of bowl.	Snow blanket (*kiapawe*). A prayer for snow, especially for women who want their gardens damp.	Diamond inside the bowl (*alu-nune ettoye*). The black clouds are coming together all directions.
41	Center of bowl.	Great star. (*moweatcunlan-na*). A prayer for light during the night.	Star inside stripes (*moweatcun eton t'sipopa*). They used to paint stars on bowls so that there might be no shooting stars. Shooting stars are omens of bad luck. When

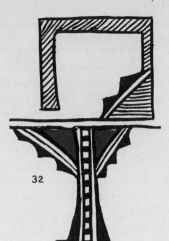

32

33

34

35

36

37

38

39

PLATE XXV

ZUNI DESIGN ELEMENTS

32-36, for bodies of jars; 37-39 for centers of bowls

No.	Use	Names and Meaning	
		1924	1925
			there is water in the bowl, the star looks in and sees its image.
42	Center of bowl.	Ceremonial blanket design (*miha ťsinanne*). A prayer for a blanket, because we think so much of the sacred blanket.	Ceremonial blanket with clouds standing up (*miha awełuya yałtopa*). This represents the dress of the masked gods.
43	Center of bowl.	Lightning between red clouds. (*wilonanne locilowa*). This represents a struggle between the red clouds (wind clouds) and the white clouds (rain clouds) with victory for rain since the white cloud is larger.	Striped feathers, red feather and square (*lapana ťsipopa, labana cilowa maiyak'okci*).
44	Inside of bowl.	Red cloud square (*maiyak'okci cilowapa*).	Striped square with downy feathers (*maiyak'okci ťsipopa*) (*lacowapa*).
45	Inside of bowl.	Ceremonial blanket design (*miha ťsinane*).	a. Red steps (*hewi'etciwe cilowa*). b. Striped steps (*hewi'etciwe ťsipopa*. c. Checked square (*mayak'okci kucoktanne*).
46	Inside of bowl.	Cloud all alone (*awełuyan samapoaye*). This is the little cloud all along in the sky after it has cleared. The people who do not go to dances are like that when they die and go to the village of the Masked Gods. When the Masked Gods come back to Itiwana, she will not be able to come with them, but will have to stay all alone like a cloud after the sky has cleared. And she will always be looking and looking for someone to come. That is why they paint eyes looking out in all directions.	a. Striped clouds (*awełuya ťsipopa*). b. Red cloud steps (*hewi'etci' cilowa*). The clouds are turning around. They are coming up fast, and they touch one another. They have all come, the black and the red and the white and the striped clouds, and they fill the sky.
47	Inside of bowl.	Lightning steps (*wilona hewi'etciwe*). Lightning steps, with birds' feather to make	a. Striped bowl design (*sa'lan ťsinanne ťsipopa*). b. Feathers (*lapanawe*). They

PLATE XXVI

Zuni design elements

40-47, for interiors of bowls

[103]

No.	Use	Names and Meaning	
		1924	1925
		the road for the birds to come in after the rain is over.	use the feathers because the clouds are not willing to come.
48	Inside of bowl.	Valuable drawing for the bowl (*sa'lan eton*). We make this for good luck.	
49	Inside of bowl.	Red clouds and black clouds make flowers grow (*awełuya cilowa awełuya kwinne utea cikwa*). A prayer that rain and snow clouds may come and make the flowers grow.	Crooks come together (*netsikâ anhapełnapa*).
50	Inside of bowl.		
51	Inside of bowl.	Black clouds hang down (*lok'winne paninapa*). Snow and rain clouds hanging down so that we may have rain.	Crooks (*netsikâwe*).
52	Inside of bowl.	Wooden Ears (*łelacoktipona*). The name of a masked god. We always like to see him come in.	Masked God's ear (*kok'wan lacoktinne*).
53	Inside of bowl, neck or body of.	Butterfly standing up in a cloud (*pulakia awełuyanne elayałtoye*). A prayer for a beautiful summer with butterflies and clouds.	Dragon fly standing up in the clouds and calling the rain (*cumaikolowe*).
54	Inside of bowl.		a. Crooks standing up (*netsikâwe elaye*). b. Cloud triangle (*nitebowa awełuya*).
55	Inside of bowl or side of jar.	a. Rainbow carrying the clouds (*amitolạnne awełuyanne haktonan*). b. Arrow points (cloud heads) c. Crooks. We believe that a rainbow stops rain. So that this may not happen, the clouds are placed above the rainbow.	a. A wall in the cloud house. b. Yucca suds. c. Flowers. This is a prayer for hunting, that the deer may come in and the hunters have good luck in killing them.
56	Inside of bowl.	Earth with flowers (*awi'uteapa*). A prayer for a beautiful summer.	Crooks coming together (*netsikâ atc iyulipa*).
57	Inside of bowl.	Hearts with supernatural power (*tsemawanikwa ikye-*	Crooks at the edge (*netsikâ anpałtopa*). This is like the

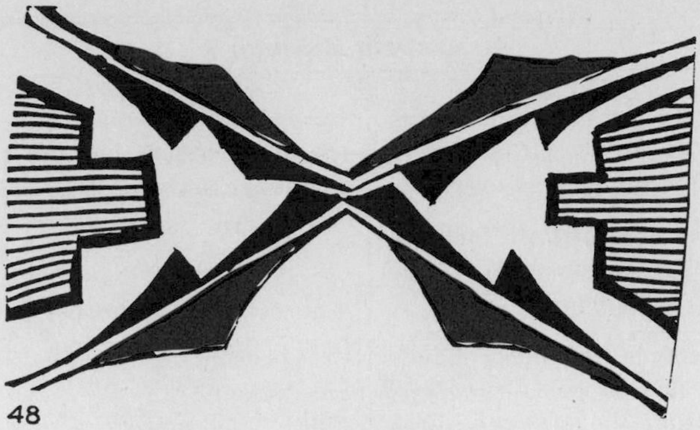

PLATE XXVII
ZUNI DESIGN ELEMENTS
48-55, for interiors of bowls

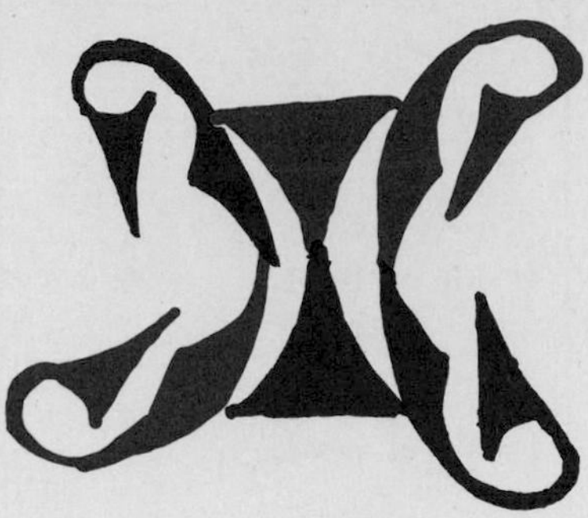

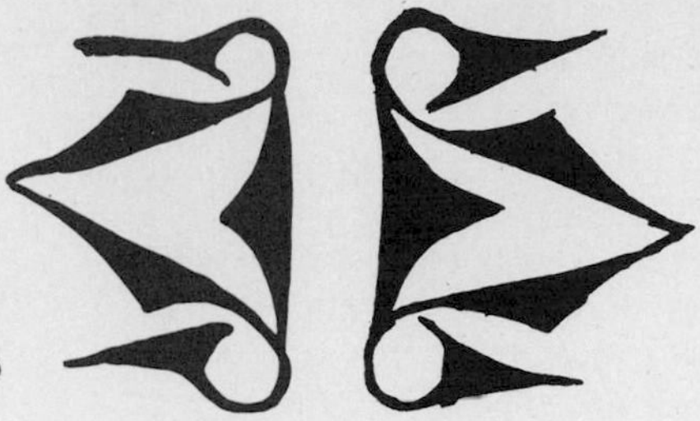

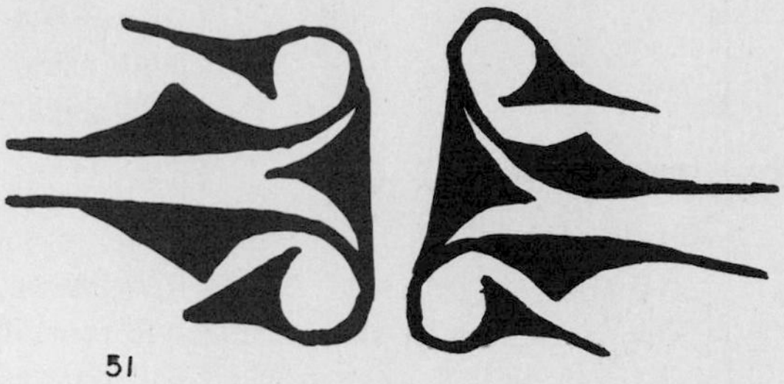

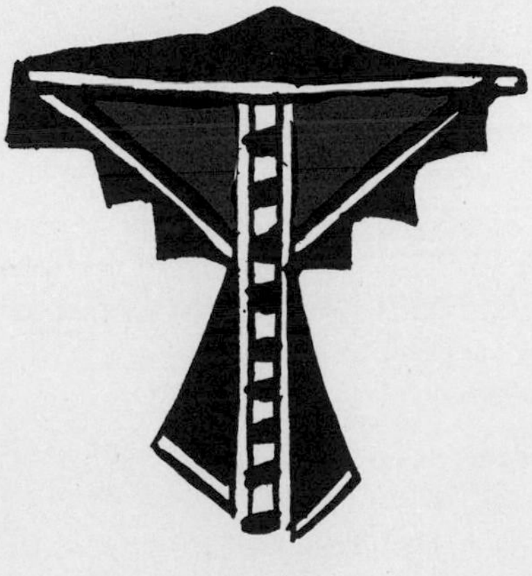

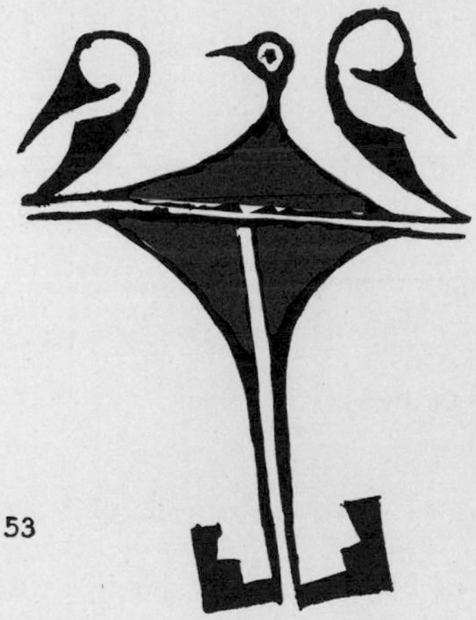

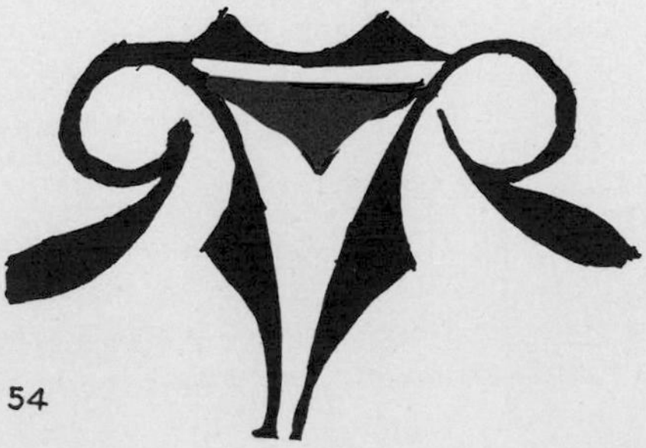

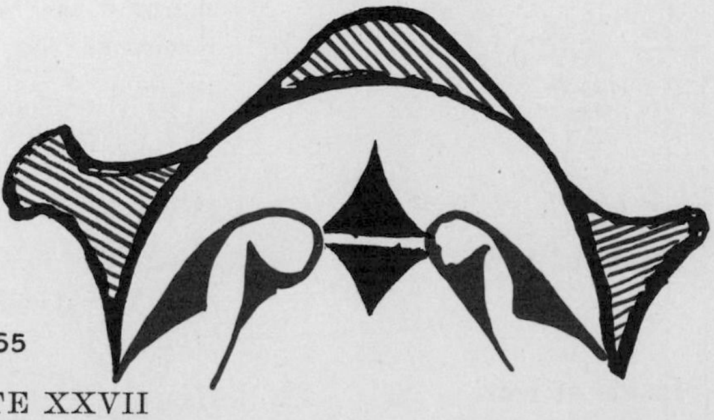

No.	Use	Names and Meaning	
		1924	1925
		nawe). These are the hearts of the Beast Gods and the crooks used by the Society people.	painting of some of the katcina masks that have lines around the faces.
58	Inside of bowl.	Feathers and downy feathers (*lapana laconapa*). Prayer sticks with downy feathers for the rain. My husband's prayers were not answered, so I make this prayer, like planting prayer sticks.	Butterfly with downy feathers (*pulakia lacowapa*). This is the butterfly used by the katcinas to lure people to the dance.
59	Outside of bowl.		Red downy feather (*lacowapa cilowa*).
60	Outside rim of bowls. "It is always placed on the outside so that it will show even when the bowl is full.	Feathers (*lapanawe*). The Rain makers are the spirits of the dead Zunis, and whenever anyone dies they plant feathers. Women do not prepare prayersticks, and that is why we always put feathers on the jars. It is the same as planting feathers outside for the dead.	Feathers (*lapanawe*).
61	Outside of bowl.	All different kinds of clouds hang down (*lotemła wohanapa*). A prayer that all kinds of clouds may gather together and make a cloudy day.	Striped clouds (*awełuya ťsipopa*) and tail feathers (*lakwelenawe*).
62	Outside of bowl or neck of jar.	Red and black cloud steps with lightning (*hewi'etciwe cilowa lowe k'winne wilonanapa*). Steps for the rain to come down. Lightning always makes the rain come fast. A prayer for rain.	Feathers (*labanawe*).
63	Outside of bowl.	Feathers meeting face to face (*lawe iyaniktocnapa*).	Long flowers (*utea tomatcawe*).
64	Outside of bowl.	Labyrinth (*ona'ilacnapa*). A prayer that the Navaho may not find us in war. A prayer for safety.	Black steps (*hewi'etci k'winne*). This is for the clouds, and the diagonal lines (black) are to keep the clouds from coming together.
65	Outside of bowl.	Marking on the road (*onawa ťsinapa*). A broken trail. The	Black cloud steps (*hewi'etci k'winne*). This is the same as

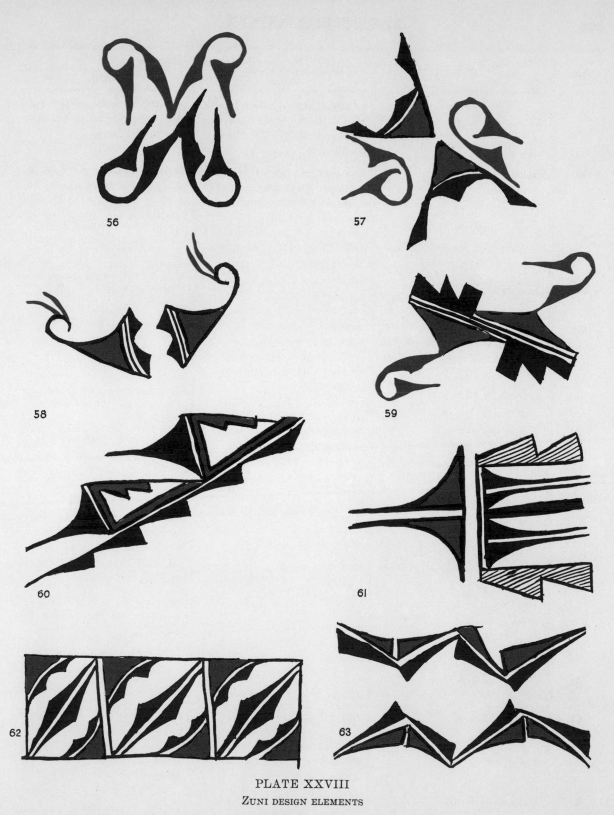

PLATE XXVIII
Zuni design elements

56-58, for centers of bowls; 59-63, for outer rims of bowls

No.	Use	Names and Meaning	
		1924	1925
		pursuers do not know which way to go. A prayer for safety in war. (Roads are blocked by lines of cornmeal.)	No. 64. It means the same thing, but it has the red clouds also.
66	Inside rim of bowl.	Zig-zag (*wetolianne*) or waves (*ałialaye*), or water-snake (*citola*).	Waves stand up (*wetolian łuwalaye*).
67	Inside rim of bowl.	Straight line; cloud in sky (*'upiłane*). This is a prayer for rain.	Cloud steps coming together (*hewi'etciwe iyaniktocnapa*).
68	Inside rim of bowl.	Road black for witches (*ona k'winne opimaiya*). A prayer that one's road may be protected from witches. A common greeting is "*opimaiya onak'winne*," may your road be hidden from witches.	Cloud steps going up (*hewi'etci yemaktcełnapa*).
69	Inside rim of bowl.	Feathers (*lapanawe*).	Feathers meeting face to face (*lapana iyaniktocnapa*).
70	Inside rim of bowl.	Little clouds and rainbow (*sułayawe amitolanne*). A prayer to stop rain because pots do not fire well in the rain. The rainbow cuts the clouds apart and stops the rain.	Striped cloud steps with Milky Way in the middle (*hewi'etciwe t'sipa kucoktapa itiwa*). The steps are the clouds. They are coming together from the east and the west, but the Milky Way comes between them, so that it may not rain. The witches call the Milky Way to come and prevent rain.
71	Inside rim of bowl or neck of jars.	Red neck (*witcicilowa*).	Cloud steps and triangle for neck (*hewietciwe nitepowa witci*).
72	Inside rim of bowl or neck of jar.		Cloud steps (*hewi'etciwe*).
73	Inside rim of bowl.	Prayer bow (*t'ewusu pi'łane*). A prayer, like meeting for prayer (*t'ewusu*), i.e. going into retreat.	Bow with downy feathers (*pi'ła lacowapa*).
74	Inside rim of bowl.	All different kinds of flowers (*utea wotemłananawe*). A prayer for a beautiful summer.	Flower design (*utean t'sinan*). They make this so that there may be many flowers.

64

65

66

67

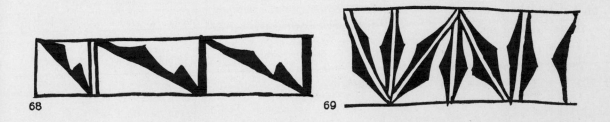

68

69

70

71

PLATE XXIX
Zuni design elements
64, 65, for the outer rims of bowls; 66-71, for the inner rims of bowls

No.	Use	Names and Meaning	
		1924	1925
75	Neck of jar.	Bow with downy feathers (*pi'ła lacowapa*).	Two bows with downy feathers (*pi'ła atci lacowapa*). This is for the katcinas.
76	Rim of jar, always with 77; sometimes used in vertical panel on body.	Diamond (*ałununanne*) and *neweyulinne*. The diamond represents the bird sling used by boys. *Neweyulinne* is the face painting of the Newekwe society. The face is covered with ashes and the design is put around the mouth with black pigment.	Baby ornament (*wihapatci*). This is to bring good luck in childhood. It is unfinished, like a child in the mother's womb.
77	Neck of jar, always with No. 76.	Stripes with points; triangle (*t'sipopa kyatsotanne*). This represents the thunder-knife (*timuci*) which the priests use in many ceremonies.	a. Feathers sticking up (*lakwelenapa*). b. Clouds (*awełuyawe*). c. Feather for head (*labanawe*). d. Crook (*netsikânne*). e. Square (*maiyak'okci*) like the painting on the mask of Ko'kokci. The whole design is called feathers (*labanawe*).
78	Neck of jar.	Diamond with feathers (*ałununu lapopa*).	Square with feathers (*maiya kokci'labanapa*).
79 A	Used together on neck of jars.	Crook with stripes (*netsikâwe tsipopa*). The crook is the ceremonial drumstick; the hatching represents falling rain; the broad stripe with black dots represents the perfect ear of corn, painted that the crops may be plentiful.	Crook with stripes (*netsi kânne tsipopa*).
79 B	Used on neck of jars always with No. 77 A.	Feather painting (*lakwelena*).	Feathers (*lakwelena*).
80	Neck of jar.	Mountain goat horns (*haliku saiyawe*).	Striped mountain goat horns (*halik'wan saiyawe t'sipopa*).
81	Neck of jar.	Cloud with downy feathers (*awełuyan lacowapa*). A prayer that a person may come back after death with the rain and thunder. We put the head in the clouds to show that it is a person. The clouds are the dead.	Feathers tied together hanging down on the neck (*lapsimone witcin*).

PLATE XXX

ZUNI DESIGN ELEMENTS

72-74, for the inner rims of bowls; 75-79, for the necks of jars

No.	Use	Names and Meaning	
		1924	1925
82	Neck of jar.	Arrow head ornament and scrolls (*heakwin patci, wikone*).	a. Striped mountain goat horn (*saiyanne halikan t'sipopa*). b. Drumstick with downy feathers (*netsikânne lacowapa*). c. Head-dress of masked god maidens (*matsikwanne*).
83	Used neck of jar.	Inchworm (*colowapa*). We paint it because it lives around springs.	An inchworm (*colowapa*). The inchworm comes out after the rain and therefore we paint them in order to have rain.
84	Used on neck of jars, also in bowls.	Butterfly (*pulakia*).	Butterfly (*pulakia*). Standing up with cloud feet. He is like the black clouds.
85	Not specified.	Turkey tracks (*tonna teananne*). Once a girl came home late from the Yaya dance and found her neglected turkeys gone. The people of Itiwana had bad luck because they needed the turkey feathers for their prayer-sticks. So they followed their tracks and made this design to bring them back.	Turkey wings (*ton'an asinne*). We paint the tracks of the turkey because we use turkey feathers.
86	Not specified.	Thin unhappy little clouds (*sulahaiya kwa ikyen k'okcame*). The snow clouds (black) and the rain clouds (red) are fighting. Therefore there will be no rain.	Long feathers coming together (*lahatacan ihapełnapa*).
87	Not specified.	Snow cloud meets the rain cloud (*upinakia lonawe łitokia lonawe tsula'ate*). A prayer that the rain may not melt the snow clouds.	Lone star with clouds (*moweatacun'awełuyapa*).
88	Not specified.	Ancient head-dress of girls. (*matsikânne*). The women like the way the katcina maidens do their hair and so make a picture of it.	Ancient head-dress of girls. (*matsikânne*); with torquoise and a red feather.
89	Not specified.	Clouds struggling with rainbow. (*lowe amitolan anipewenawe*). The rainbow tries	Masked god's painting (*kokwan politan*). The painting on the mask of Kowo łanna.

PLATE XXXI

ZUNI DESIGN ELEMENTS

80-84, for the necks of jars; 85-87, use not specified

[113]

No.	Use	Names and Meaning	
		1924	1925
		to stop rain, but the clouds come over it, and so it will rain in spite of everything. A prayer for rain in unfavorable conditions.	
90	Not specified.	Arrow points meeting (*heakwin'iyaniktocnapa*). The arrow points on both sides meet and fighting stops. Darkness comes and stops the fighting. A prayer for the end of war.	Arrows come together (*timuci'ihapełnapa*). Long ago we used to fight, but we do not want any more fighting. When the arrows come together, it is as if the fighting stopped.
91	Not specified.	Two rainbows (*kwili amitolawe*).	
92	Not specified.	Double cloud steps (*hewi'etciwe iyałtopa*).	Cloud steps with feathers (*hewi'etciwe lapanapa*).
93	Not specified.	Stars in a dark sky (*moweatcu wopapa*).	Two diamonds with feathers (*lapanawe ałununu'atci*).
94	Not specified.		

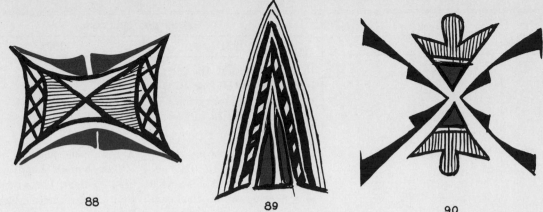

88　　　　　　89　　　　　　90

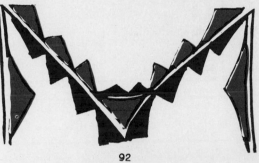

91　　　　　　　92

93　　　　　　　94

PLATE XXXII

Zuni design elements

88-94, use not specified

[115]

APPENDIX II

HOPI DESIGNS

1

2

3

4

5

6

7

8

PLATE XXXIII

HOPI DESIGNS FOR INTERIORS OF BOWLS, DRAWN BY NATIVE ARTIST

[118]

PLATE XXXIV

HOPI DESIGNS, DRAWN BY NATIVE ARTIST

9-12, for interiors of bowls: 13-15, complete design for a bowl (13, inner border; 14, center; 15, outer border); 16-19, borders for exteriors of bowls or jars

APPENDIX III

SAN ILDEFONSO DESIGNS

APPENDIX III

SAN ILDEFONSO DESIGNS

No.	JULIAN	ABEL	JUAN
1	*Avanyu.*	*Avanyu.*	*Avanyu.*
2			Clouds come down.
3	a. Drops. b. Clouds.	Clouds and rain.	Cloud flowers. The clouds look like flowers when they come out from behind the mountains.
4		a. Wind clouds. b. Clouds.	White clouds.
5		Clouds and rain.	Spotted cloud.
6		Clouds and rain.	Wind cloud.
7		Clouds blown in the same direction.	Clouds waving.
8		Clouds going in the same direction.	(Did not know.)
9			Fog.
10			
11			Gray cloud.
12			
13	a, a. Birds. b. Another bird, or clouds.		Cloud steps.
14	a. Wing. b. Clouds. c. Leaf.	Wind clouds meeting.	Clouds passing.
15			Owl's eye.
16			Nose of the clouds.
17	a. Leaf. b. Cloud.	Clouds and rain going in two directions.	Fog standing.

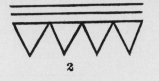

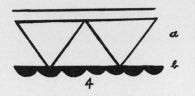

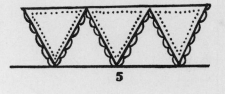

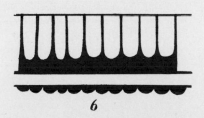

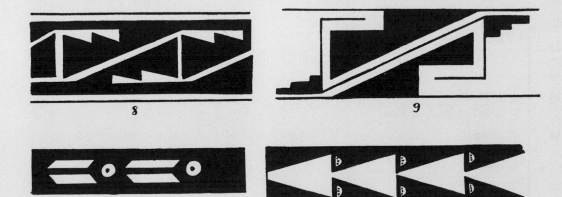

PLATE XXXV

SAN ILDEFONSO DESIGNS

1-11, continuous borders for small bowls

No.	JULIAN	ABEL	JUAN
18	a, a. Bird. b. Another bird. c. Cloud. d. Clouds and hail stones.	Clouds and rain going in two ways.	Yellow fog.
19		Wind clouds and rain clouds and rain.	Clouds meeting.
20	a. Bird. b. Tail. c. Clouds.	Clouds and rain.	Clouds meeting.
21	Bird.		Clouds lying down.
22			Clouds standing.
23			Clouds in row, cloud steps.
24	a. Bird. b. Clouds.		Cloud tail.
25	a. Bird. b. Cloud. c. Leaf.	a. Wind clouds. b. Rain.	Cloud standing.
26	a. Cloud. b. Leaf. c. Rain.	Clouds send rain, going in two directions.	Clouds bringing showers.
27			
28	The whole thing is a bird: a. Steps. b. Leaf. d. Tail. d. Clouds.	a. Pueblo. b. Wind clouds. c. Wind clouds. d. Clouds. e. Rain clouds.	 Clouds passing.
29	a. Leaf. b. Tail.		
30			Dark cloud.
31			
32 33 34	The three together are called "nice design." 32—Rain. 33—a. Clouds. b. Hailstones. c. Wing. 34—a. Steps. b. Houses.	Clouds standing.	Red cloud.
35			
36			

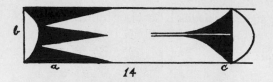

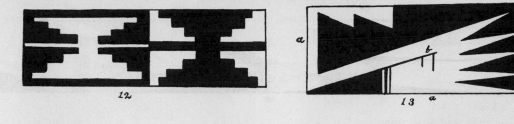

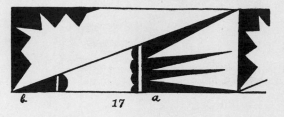

PLATE XXXVI

San Ildefonso designs

12-23, panelled borders for small bowls

[125]

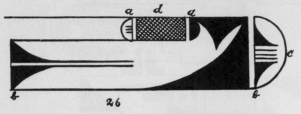

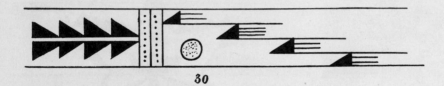

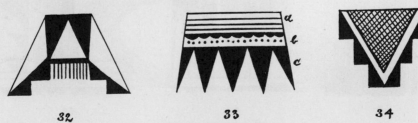

PLATE XXXVII

Sᴀɴ Iʟᴅᴇꜰᴏɴꜱᴏ ᴅᴇꜱɪɢɴꜱ

24-31, borders for small bowls; 32-34, three units of border of small bowl.

[126]

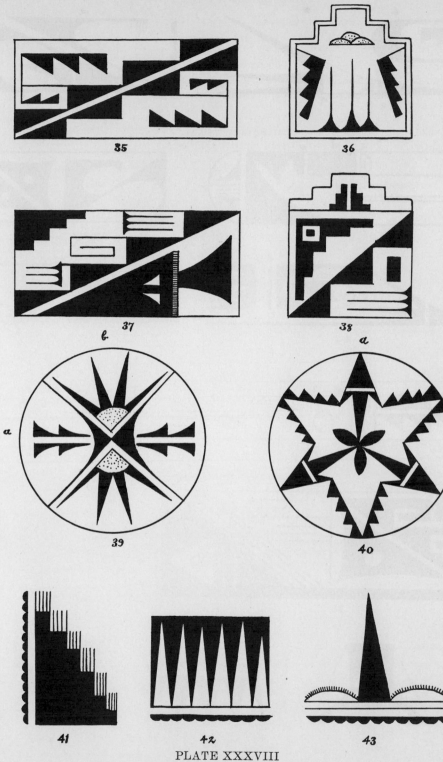

PLATE XXXVIII

S<small>AN</small> I<small>LDEFONSO</small> <small>DESIGNS</small>

35, 36, side and end of rectangular box; 37, 38, side and end of rectangular box; 39, 40, designs for
small plates; 41-43, deep borders for vases

[127]

No.	JULIAN	ABEL	JUAN
37 38		Eagle feathers, with rain and clouds and wind.	37. Clouds on the mountain. 38. Clouds come out.
39	a. Turkey tail. b. Leaf.	In the center, wind cloud with rain drops; the rest is little clouds.	Clouds shining.
40	Whole design called star. a. Leaf. b. Steps.	Star with clouds.	Star.
41		A pueblo with rain.	Light clouds, rain clouds.
42			Black cloud.
43		Clouds with rain drops and with a wind cloud in the center.	Rain clouds.

BIBLIOGRAPHY

BOAS, FRANZ. The Decorative Art of the Indians of the North Pacific Coast. *Bulletin of the American Museum of Natural History*, Vol. IX, pp. 123-176. New York, 1897.

—— The Decorative Art of the North American Indians. *Popular Science Monthly*, October, 1903.

—— Primitive Art. Guide Leaflet No. 15, *American Museum Journal*, Vol. IV, No. 3. New York, 1904.

—— Primitive Art. Cambridge, Mass., 1927.

CUSHING, FRANK HAMILTON. Zuni Fetishes. *Second Annual Report, Bureau of American Ethnology*, pp. 3-45. Washington, 1883.

—— A Study of Pueblo Pottery as Illustrative of Zuni Culture Growth. *Fourth Annual Report, Bureau of American Ethnology*, pp. 467-521. Washington, 1886.

—— Zuni Breadstuffs. *Indian Notes and Monographs. Museum of the American Indian Heye Foundation*. New York, 1920.

DIXON, R. B. Basketry Designs of the Indians of Northern California. *Bulletin of the American Museum of Natural History*, Vol. XVII. New York,

EMMONS, GEORGE THORNTON AND FRANZ BOAS. The Chilkat Blanket. *Memoirs of American Museum of Natural History*. Vol. III, New York, 1907.

—— The Basketry of the Tlingit. Ibid.

FEWKES, J. WALTER. Tusayan Katcinas. *Fifteenth Annual Report of the Bureau of American Ethnology*, pp. 39-48. Washington, 1897.

—— Archaeological Expedition to Arizona, 1895. *Seventeenth Annual Report of the Bureau of American Ethnology*, pp. 519-744. Washington, 1901.

—— Hopi Katcinas, *Twenty-first Annual Report of the Bureau of American Ethnology*, pp. 3-126. Washington, 1903.

—— Two Summers' Work in Pueblo Ruins, *Twenty-second Annual Report of the Bureau of American Ethnology*, pp. 3-195. Washington, 1903.

—— Ancient Zuni Pottery, Putnam Anniversary Vol., pp. 43-82. New York, 1909.

—— Antiquities of Mesa Verde National Park, Spruce Tree House, *Forty-first Annual Report of the Bureau of American Ethnology*. Washington, 1909.

—— Antiquities of Mesa Verde National Park, Cliff Palace. *Fifty-first Annual Report of the Bureau of American Ethnology*. Washington, 1911.

—— Designs in Prehistoric Hopi Pottery, *Thirty-third Annual Report of the Bureau of American Ethnology*, pp. 207-284. Washington, 1919.

—— Design on Prehistoric Pottery from Mimbres Valley, New Mexico. *Smithsonian Miscellaneous Collections*, Vol. 74, No. 6. Washington, 1923.

GODDARD, P. E. Indians of the Southwest. *American Museum of Natural History Handbook Series*. New York, 1921.

GUTHE, CARL E. Pueblo Pottery Making. *Publications of the Department of Archaeology, Phillips Academy, Andover*. New Haven. 1925.

HADDON, ALFRED CORT. Evolution in Art. London. W. Scott, Ltd. 1914.

HAEBERLIN, H. K., TEIT, JAMES, and ROBERTS, HELEN H., Coiled Basketry in British Columbia, *Forty-first Annual Report of the Bureau of American Ethnology*. Washington, 1928.

HODGE, F. W. Pottery of Hawikuh. *Indian Notes, Museum of the American Indian, Heye Foundation*, Vol. I, No. 1, pp. 8-15. New York, 1924.

—— Circular Kivas near Hawikuh, New Mexico. *Contributions from the Museum of the American Indian, Heye Foundation*, Vol. VII, No. 1. New York, 1923.

HOLMES, WILLIAM H. Illustrated Catalogue of a Portion of the Collections made by the Bureau of Ethnology during the Field Season of 1881. *Third Annual Report of the Bureau of American Ethnology*, pp. 427-510. Washington, 1884.

—— Ancient Pottery of the Mississippi Valley. *Fourth Annual Report of the Bureau of American Ethnology*, pp. 361-436. Washington, 1886.

—— Pottery of the Ancient Pueblos. *Fourth Annual Report of the Bureau of American Ethnology*, pp. 257-360. Washington, 1886.

—— Origin and Development of Form and Ornament in Ceramic Art. *Fourth Annual Report of the Bureau of American Ethnology*, pp. 437-465. Washington, 1886.

—— Study of Textile Art in its Relation to Form and Ornament. *Sixth Annual Report of the Bureau of American Ethnology*, pp. 189-252. Washington, 1888.

—— Aboriginal Pottery of the Eastern United States. *Twentieth Annual Report of the Bureau of American Ethnology*, pp. 1-201. Washington, 1903.

HOUGH, WALTER. Antiquities of Upper Gila and Salt River Valleys in Arizona and New Mexico. *Thirty-fifth Annual Report of the Bureau of American Ethnology*, Washington, 1907.

KIDDER, A. V. Pottery of Pajarito Plateau and Some Adjacent Regions in New Mexico. *Memoirs of the American Anthropological Association*. Lancaster, Pa., 1915.

—— An Introduction to the Study of Southwestern Archaeology. *Publications of the Department of Archaeology of Phillips Academy, Andover*. New Haven, 1924.

KIDDER, A. V. AND M. A. Notes on the Pottery of Pecos. *American Anthropologist* N. S., Vol. 19, No. 3, pp. 325-360. Lancaster, Pa., 1917.

KIDDER, A. V. AND GUERNSEY, S. J. Archaeological Explorations in Northeastern Arizona. *Sixty-fifth Annual Report of the Bureau of American Ethnology*. Washington, 1919.

KROEBER, A. L. The Arapaho. *Bulletin of American Museum of Natural History*, Vol. XVIII. New York, 1902.

NELSON, N. C. Pueblo Ruins of the Galisteo Basin, New Mexico. *Anthropological Papers, American Museum of Natural History*, Vol. XV, Pt. 1, New York. 1914.

—— Chronology of Tano Ruins, New Mexico. *American Anthropologist* N. S., Vol. 18, No. 2, pp. 159-180. Lancaster, Pa., 1916.

NORDENSKEOLD, G. The Cliff Dwellers of the Mesa Verde. Stockholm, 1893.

ORCHARD, W. C. Fine Line Decoration of Ancient Southwestern pottery. *Indian Notes, Museum of American Indian Heye Foundation*, New York, 1925.

SPIER, LESLIE. An outline for a chronology of Zuni Ruins. *Anthropological Papers, American Museum of Natural History*, Vol. XVIII, Pt. 3. New York, 1917.

—— Notes on some little Colorado Ruins. *Anthropological Papers, American Museum of Natural History*, Vol. XVIII, p. 4. New York, 1918.

STEVENSON, MATHILDE COXE. The Zuni Indians. *Twenty-third Annual Report of the Bureau of American Ethnology*, pp. 1-608. Washington, 1904.

STEVENSON, JAMES. Illustrated Catalogue of the Collection Obtained from the Indians of New Mexico. *Second Annual Report of the Bureau of American Ethnology*, pp. 423-465, Washington, 1883.

—— Illustrated Catalogue of Collections Obtained from Indians of New Mexico and Arizona in 1879. *Second Annual Report of Bureau of American Ethnology*, pp. 307-422. Washington, 1883.

—— Illustrated Catalogue of the Collections obtained from the Pueblos of Zuni, New Mexico, and Walpi, Arizona, in 1881. *Third Annual Report of the Bureau of American Ethnology*, pp. 511-514. Washington, 1884.

INDEX

INDEX

Dover Books on Art

PRINCIPLES OF ART HISTORY, H. Wölfflin. This remarkably instructive work demonstrates the tremendous change in artistic conception from the 14th to the 18th centuries, by analyzing 164 works by Botticelli, Dürer, Hobbema, Holbein, Hals, Titian, Rembrandt, Vermeer, etc., and pointing out exactly what is meant by "baroque," "classic," "primitive," "picturesque," and other basic terms of art history and criticism. "A remarkable lesson in the art of seeing," SAT. REV. OF LITERATURE. Translated from the 7th German edition. 150 illus. 254pp. 6⅛ x 9¼. 20276-3 Paperbound $2.50

FOUNDATIONS OF MODERN ART, A. Ozenfant. Stimulating discussion of human creativity from paleolithic cave painting to modern painting, architecture, decorative arts. Fully illustrated with works of Gris, Lipchitz, Léger, Picasso, primitive, modern artifacts, architecture, industrial art, much more. 226 illustrations. 368pp. 6⅛ x 9¼. 20215-1 Paperbound $3.00

METALWORK AND ENAMELLING, H. Maryon. Probably the best book ever written on the subject. Tells everything necessary for the home manufacture of jewelry, rings, ear pendants, bowls, etc. Covers materials, tools, soldering, filigree, setting stones, raising patterns, repoussé work, damascening, niello, cloisonné, polishing, assaying, casting, and dozens of other techniques. The best substitute for apprenticeship to a master metalworker. 363 photos and figures. 374pp. 5½ x 8½.
20183-X Clothbound $8.50

SHAKER FURNITURE, E. D. and *F. Andrews.* The most illuminating study of Shaker furniture ever written. Covers chronology, craftsmanship, houses, shops, etc. Includes over 200 photographs of chairs, tables, clocks, beds, benches, etc. "Mr. & Mrs. Andrews know all there is to know about Shaker furniture," Mark Van Doren, NATION. 48 full-page plates. 192pp. 7⅞ x 10¾. 20679-3 Paperbound $2.75

LETTERING AND ALPHABETS, J. A. Cavanagh. An unabridged reissue of "Lettering," containing the full discussion, analysis, illustration of 89 basic hand lettering styles based on Caslon, Bodoni, Gothic, many other types. Hundreds of technical hints on construction, strokes, pens, brushes, etc. 89 alphabets, 72 lettered specimens, which may be reproduced permission-free. 121pp. 9¾ x 8. 20053-1 Paperbound $1.50

THE HUMAN FIGURE IN MOTION, Eadweard Muybridge. The largest collection in print of Muybridge's famous high-speed action photos. 4789 photographs in more than 500 action-strip-sequences (at shutter speeds up to 1/6000th of a second) illustrate men, women, children—mostly undraped—performing such actions as walking, running, getting up, lying down, carrying objects, throwing, etc. "An unparalleled dictionary of action for all artists," AMERICAN ARTIST. 390 full-page plates, with 4789 photographs. Heavy glossy stock, reinforced binding with headbands. 7⅞ x 10¾. 20204-6 Clothbound $12.50

AFRICAN SCULPTURE, Ladislas Segy. 163 full-page plates illustrating masks, fertility figures, ceremonial objects, etc., of 50 West and Central African tribes—95% never before illustrated. 34-page introduction to African sculpture. "Mr. Segy is one of its top authorities," NEW YORKER. 164 full-page photographic plates. Introduction. Bibliography. 244pp. 6⅛ x 9¼.

20396-4 Paperbound $2.25

CALLIGRAPHY, J. G. Schwandner. First reprinting in 200 years of this legendary book of beautiful handwriting. Over 300 ornamental initials, 12 complete calligraphic alphabets, over 150 ornate frames and panels, 75 calligraphic pictures of cherubs, stags, lions, etc., thousands of flourishes, scrolls, etc., by the greatest 18th-century masters. All material can be copied or adapted without permission. Historical introduction. 158 full-page plates. 368pp. 9 x 13. 20475-8 Clothbound $10.00

PRINTED EPHEMERA, edited and collected by John Lewis. This book contains centuries of design, typographical and pictorial motives in proven, effective commercial layouts. Hundreds of the most striking examples of labels, tickets, posters, wrappers, programs, menus, and other items have been collected in this handsome and useful volume, along with information on the dimensions and colors of the original, printing processes used, stylistic notes on typography and design, etc. Study this book and see how the best commercial artists of the past and present have solved their particular problems. Most of the material is copyright free. 713 illustrations, many in color. Illustrated index of type faces included. Glossary of technical terms. Indexes. 288pp. 9¼ x 12. 22284-5, 22285-3 Clothbound $15.00

DESIGN FOR ARTISTS AND CRAFTSMEN, Louis Wolchonok. Recommended for either individual or classroom use, this book helps you to create original designs from things about you, from geometric patterns, from plants, animals, birds, humans, landscapes, manmade objects. "A great contribution," N. Y. Society of Craftsmen. 113 exercises with hints and diagrams. More than 1280 illustrations. xv + 207pp. 7⅞ x 10¾.

20274-7 Paperbound $2.75

HANDBOOK OF ORNAMENT, F. S. Meyer. One of the largest collections of copyright-free traditional art: over 3300 line cuts of Greek, Roman, Medieval, Renaissance, Baroque, 18th and 19th century art motifs (tracery, geometric elements, flower and animal motifs, etc.) and decorated objects (chairs, thrones, weapons, vases, jewelry, armor, etc.). Full text. 300 plates. 3300 illustrations. 562pp. 5⅜ x 8. 20302-6 Paperbound $2.75

THREE CLASSICS OF ITALIAN CALLIGRAPHY, Oscar Ogg, ed. Exact reproductions of three famous Renaissance calligraphic works: Arrighi's OPERINA and IL MODO, Tagliente's LO PRESENTE LIBRO, and Palatino's LIBRO NUOVO. More than 200 complete alphabets, thousands of lettered specimens, in Papal Chancery and other beautiful, ornate handwriting. Introduction. 245 plates. 282pp. 6⅛ x 9¼. 20212-7 Paperbound $2.75

ART ANATOMY, Dr. William Rimmer. One of the few books on art anatomy that are themselves works of art, this is a faithful reproduction (rearranged for handy use) of the extremely rare masterpiece of the famous 19th century anatomist, sculptor, and art teacher. Beautiful, clear line drawings show every part of the body—bony structure, muscles, features, etc. Unusual are the sections on falling bodies, foreshortenings, muscles in tension, grotesque personalities, and Rimmer's remarkable interpretation of emotions and personalities as expressed by facial features. It will supplement every other book on art anatomy you are likely to have. Reproduced clearer than the lithographic original (which sells for $500 on up on the rare book market.) Over 1,200 illustrations. xiii + 153pp. 7¾ x 10¾.

20908-3 Paperbound $2.50

THE CRAFTSMAN'S HANDBOOK, Cennino Cennini. The finest English translation of IL LIBRO DELL' ARTE, the 15th century introduction to art technique that is both a mirror of Quatrocento life and a source of many useful but nearly forgotten facets of the painter's art. 4 illustrations. xxvii + 142pp. D. V. Thompson, translator. 5⅜ x 8. 20054-X Paperbound $1.75

THE BROWN DECADES, Lewis Mumford. A picture of the "buried renaissance" of the post-Civil War period, and the founding of modern architecture (Sullivan, Richardson, Root, Roebling), landscape development (Marsh, Olmstead, Eliot), and the graphic arts (Homer, Eakins, Ryder). 2nd revised, enlarged edition. Bibliography. 12 illustrations. xiv + 266 pp. 5⅜ x 8.

20200-3 Paperbound $2.00

THE STYLES OF ORNAMENT, A. Speltz. The largest collection of line ornament in print, with 3750 numbered illustrations arranged chronologically from Egypt, Assyria, Greeks, Romans, Etruscans, through Medieval, Renaissance, 18th century, and Victorian. No permissions, no fees needed to use or reproduce illustrations. 400 plates with 3750 illustrations. Bibliography. Index. 640pp. 6 x 9. 20577-6 Paperbound $3.00

THE ART OF ETCHING, E. S. Lumsden. Every step of the etching process from essential materials to completed proof is carefully and clearly explained, with 24 annotated plates exemplifying every technique and approach discussed. The book also features a rich survey of the art, with 105 annotated plates by masters. Invaluable for beginner to advanced etcher. 374pp. 5⅜ x 8. 20049-3 Paperbound $2.75

OF THE JUST SHAPING OF LETTERS, Albrecht Dürer. This remarkable volume reveals Albrecht Dürer's rules for the geometric construction of Roman capitals and the formation of Gothic lower case and capital letters, complete with construction diagrams and directions. Of considerable practical interest to the contemporary illustrator, artist, and designer. Translated from the Latin text of the edition of 1535 by R. T. Nichol. Numerous letterform designs, construction diagrams, illustrations. iv + 43pp. 7⅛ x 10¾. 21306-4 Paperbound $1.25

MASTERPIECES OF FURNITURE, Verna Cook Salomonsky.
Photographs and measured drawings of some of the finest examples of Colonial American, 17th century English, Windsor, Sheraton, Hepplewhite, Chippendale, Louis XIV, Queen Anne, and various other furniture styles. The textual matter includes information on traditions, characteristics, background, etc. of various pieces. 101 plates. Bibliography. 224pp. 7⅞ x 10¾.

21381-1 Paperbound $3.00

PRIMITIVE ART, Franz Boas. In this exhaustive volume, a great American anthropologist analyzes all the fundamental traits of primitive art, covering the formal element in art, representative art, symbolism, style, literature, music, and the dance. Illustrations of Indian embroidery, paleolithic paintings, woven blankets, wing and tail designs, totem poles, cutlery, earthenware, baskets and many other primitive objects and motifs. Over 900 illustrations. 376pp. 5⅜ x 8.   20025-6 Paperbound $2.50

AN INTRODUCTION TO A HISTORY OF WOODCUT, A. M. Hind. Nearly all of this authoritative 2-volume set is devoted to the 15th century—the period during which the woodcut came of age as an important art form. It is the most complete compendium of information on this period, the artists who contributed to it, and their technical and artistic accomplishments. Profusely illustrated with cuts by 15th century masters, and later works for comparative purposes. 484 illustrations. 5 indexes. Total of xi + 838pp. 5⅜ x 8½. Two-vols. 20952-0, 20953-0 Paperbound $7.00

A HISTORY OF ENGRAVING AND ETCHING, A. M. Hind. Beginning with the anonymous masters of 15th century engraving, this highly regarded and thorough survey carries you through Italy, Holland, and Germany to the great engravers and beginnings of etching in the 16th century, through the portrait engravers, master etchers, practicioners of mezzotint, crayon manner and stipple, aquatint, color prints, to modern etching in the period just prior to World War I. Beautifully illustrated —sharp clear prints on heavy opaque paper. Author's preface. 3 appendixes. 111 illustrations. xviii + 487 pp. 5⅜ x 8½.

20954-7 Paperbound $3.50

ART STUDENTS' ANATOMY, E. J. Farris. Teaching anatomy by using chiefly living objects for illustration, this study has enjoyed long popularity and success in art courses and home-study programs. All the basic elements of the human anatomy are illustrated in minute detail, diagrammed and pictured as they pass through common movements and actions. 158 drawings, photographs, and roentgenograms. Glossary of anatomical terms. x + 159pp. 5⅝ x 8⅜.   20744-7 Paperbound $1.50

COLONIAL LIGHTING, A. H. Hayward. The only book to cover the fascinating story of lamps and other lighting devices in America. Beginning with rush light holders used by the early settlers, it ranges through the elaborate chandeliers of the Federal period, illustrating 647 lamps. Of great value to antique collectors, designers, and historians of arts and crafts. Revised and enlarged by James R. Marsh. xxxi + 198pp. 5⅝ x 8¼.

20975-X Paperbound $2.00

GREEK REVIVAL ARCHITECTURE IN AMERICA, T. Hamlin. A comprehensive study of the American Classical Revival, its regional variations, reasons for its success and eventual decline. Profusely illustrated with photos, sketches, floor plans and sections, displaying the work of almost every important architect of the time. 2 appendices. 39 figures, 94 plates containing 221 photos, 62 architectural designs, drawings, etc. 324-item classified bibliography. Index. xi + 439pp. 5⅜ x 8½.
21148-7 Paperbound $3.50

CREATIVE LITHOGRAPHY AND HOW TO DO IT, Grant Arnold. Written by a man who practiced and taught lithography for many years, this highly useful volume explains all the steps of the lithographic process from tracing the drawings on the stone to printing the lithograph, with helpful hints for solving special problems. Index. 16 reproductions of lithographs. 11 drawings. xv + 214pp. of text. 5⅜ x 8½.
21208-4 Paperbound $2.25

TEACH YOURSELF ANTIQUE COLLECTING, E. Bradford. An excellent, brief guide to collecting British furniture, silver, pictures and prints, pewter, pottery and porcelain, Victoriana, enamels, clocks or other antiques. Much background information difficult to find elsewhere. 15pp. of illus. 215pp. 7 x 4¼.
21368-4 Clothbound $2.00

PAINTING IN THE FAR EAST, L. Binyon. A study of over 1500 years of Oriental art by one of the world's outstanding authorities. The author chooses the most important masters in each period—Wu Tao-tzu, Toba Sojo, Kanaoka, Li Lung-mien, Masanobu, Okio, etc.—and examines the works, schools, and influence of each within their cultural context. 42 photographs. Sources of original works and selected bibliography. Notes including list of principal painters by periods. xx + 297pp. 6⅛ x 9¼.
20520-7 Paperbound $2.50

THE ALPHABET AND ELEMENTS OF LETTERING, F. W. Goudy. A beautifully illustrated volume on the aesthetics of letters and type faces and their history and development. Each plate consists of 15 forms of a single letter with the last plate devoted to the ampersand and the numerals. "A sound guide for all persons engaged in printing or drawing," Saturday Review. 27 full-page plates. 48 additional figures. xii + 131pp. 7⅞ x 10¾.
20792-7 Paperbound $2.25

THE COMPLETE BOOK OF SILK SCREEN PRINTING PRODUCTION, J. I. Biegeleisen. Here is a clear and complete picture of every aspect of silk screen technique and press operation—from individually operated manual presses to modern automatic ones. Unsurpassed as a guidebook for setting up shop, making shop operation more efficient, finding out about latest methods and equipment; or as a textbook for use in teaching, studying, or learning all aspects of the profession. 124 figures. Index. Bibliography. List of Supply Sources. xi + 253pp. 5⅜ x 8½.
21100-2 Paperbound $2.75

ANIMALS IN MOTION, Eadweard Muybridge. The largest collection of animal action photos in print. 34 different animals (horses, mules, oxen, goats, camels, pigs, cats, lions, gnus, deer, monkeys, eagles—and 22 others) in 132 characteristic actions. All 3919 photographs are taken in series at speeds up to 1/1600th of a second, offering artists, biologists, cartoonists a remarkable opportunity to see exactly how an ostrich's head bobs when running, how a lion puts his foot down, how an elephant's knee bends, how a bird flaps his wings, thousands of other hard-to-catch details. "A really marvellous series of plates," NATURE. 380 full-page plates. Heavy glossy stock, reinforced binding with headbands. 7⅛ x 10¾.   20203-8   Clothbound $10.00

THE BOOK OF SIGNS, R. Koch. 493 symbols—crosses, monograms, astrological, biological symbols, runes, etc.—from ancient manuscripts, cathedrals, coins, catacombs, pottery. May be reproduced permission-free. 493 illustrations by Fritz Kredel. 104pp. 6⅛ x 9¼.   20162-7   Paperbound $1.25

A HANDBOOK OF EARLY ADVERTISING ART, C. P. Hornung. The largest collection of copyright-free early advertising art ever compiled. Vol. I: 2,000 illustrations of animals, old automobiles, buildings, allegorical figures, fire engines, Indians, ships, trains, more than 33 other categories! Vol. II: Over 4,000 typographical specimens; 600 Roman, Gothic, Barnum, Old English faces; 630 ornamental type faces; hundreds of scrolls, initials, flourishes, etc. "A remarkable collection," PRINTERS' INK.

Vol. I: Pictorial Volume. Over 2000 illustrations. 256pp. 9 x 12.
                                  20122-8   Clothbound $10.00
Vol. II: Typographical Volume. Over 4000 specimens. 319pp.
9 x 12.   20123-6   Clothbound $10.00
                        Two volume set, Clothbound, only $20.00

THE UNIVERSAL PENMAN, George Bickham. Exact reproduction of beautiful 18th-century book of handwriting. 22 complete alphabets in finest English roundhand, other scripts, over 2000 elaborate flourishes, 122 calligraphic illustrations, etc. Material is copyright-free. "An essential part of any art library, and a book of permanent value," AMERICAN ARTIST. 212 plates. 224pp. 9 x 13¾.   20020-5   Clothbound $12.50

AN ATLAS OF ANATOMY FOR ARTISTS, F. Schider. This standard work contains 189 full-page plates, more than 647 illustrations of all aspects of the human skeleton, musculature, cutaway portions of the body, each part of the anatomy, hand forms, eyelids, breasts, location of muscles under the flesh, etc. 59 plates illustrate how Michelangelo, da Vinci, Goya, 15 others, drew human anatomy. New 3rd edition enlarged by 52 new illustrations by Cloquet, Barcsay. "The standard reference tool," AMERICAN LIBRARY ASSOCIATION. "Excellent," AMERICAN ARTIST. 189 plates, 647 illustrations. xxvi + 192pp. 7⅛ x 10⅝.   20241-0   Clothbound $6.50

AN ATLAS OF ANIMAL ANATOMY FOR ARTISTS, W. Ellenberger, H. Baum, H. Dittrich. The largest, richest animal anatomy for artists in English. Form, musculature, tendons, bone structure, expression, detailed cross sections of head, other features, of the horse, lion, dog, cat, deer, seal, kangaroo, cow, bull, goat, monkey, hare, many other animals. "Highly recommended," DESIGN. Second, revised, enlarged edition with new plates from Cuvier, Stubbs, etc. 288 illustrations. 153pp. 11⅜ x 9.

20082-5   Clothbound $2.75

ANIMAL DRAWING: ANATOMY AND ACTION FOR ARTISTS, C. R. Knight. 158 studies, with full accompanying text, of such animals as the gorilla, bear, bison, dromedary, camel, vulture, pelican, iguana, shark, etc., by one of the greatest modern masters of animal drawing. Innumerable tips on how to get life expression into your work. "An excellent reference work," SAN FRANCISCO CHRONICLE. 158 illustrations. 156pp. 10½ x 8½.   20426-X   Paperbound $3.00

ARCHITECTURAL AND PERSPECTIVE DESIGNS, Giuseppe Galli Bibiena. 50 imaginative scenic drawings of Giuseppe Galli Bibiena, principal theatrical engineer and architect to the Viennese court of Charles VI. Aside from its interest to art historians, students, and art lovers, there is a whole Baroque world of material in this book for the commercial artist. Portrait of Charles VI by Martin de Meytens. 1 allegorical plate. 50 additional plates. New introduction. vi + 103pp. 10⅛ x 13¼.

21263-7   Paperbound $2.50

HANDBOOK OF DESIGNS AND DEVICES, C. P. Hornung. A remarkable working collection of 1836 basic designs and variations, all copyright-free. Variations of circle, line, cross, diamond, swastika, star, scroll, shield, many more. Notes on symbolism. "A necessity to every designer who would be original without having to labor heavily," ARTIST AND ADVERTISER. 204 plates. 240pp. 5⅜ x 8.   20125-2   Paperbound $2.00

CHINESE HOUSEHOLD FURNITURE, G. N. Kates. A summary of virtually everything that is known about authentic Chinese furniture before it was contaminated by the influence of the West. The text covers history of styles, materials used, principles of design and craftsmanship, and furniture arrangement—all fully illustrated. xiii + 190pp. 5⅝ x 8½.

20958-X   Paperbound $2.00

DECORATIVE ART OF THE SOUTHWESTERN INDIANS, D. S. Sides. 300 black and white reproductions from one of the most beautiful art traditions of the primitive world, ranging from the geometric art of the Great Pueblo period of the 13th century to modern folk art. Motives from basketry, beadwork, Zuni masks, Hopi kachina dolls, Navajo sand pictures and blankets, and ceramic ware. Unusual and imaginative designs will inspire craftsmen in all media, and commercial artists may reproduce any of them without permission or payment. xviii + 101pp. 5⅝ x 8⅜.   20139-2   Paperbound $1.50

PINE FURNITURE OF EARLY NEW ENGLAND, R. H. Kettell. Over 400 illustrations, over 50 working drawings of early New England chairs, benches, beds, cupboards, mirrors, shelves, tables, other furniture esteemed for simple beauty and character. "Rich store of illustrations . . . emphasizes the individuality and varied design," ANTIQUES. 413 illustrations, 55 working drawings. 475pp. 8 x 10¾.   20145-7   Clothbound $10.00

BASIC BOOKBINDING, A. W. Lewis. Enables both beginners and experts to rebind old books or bind paperbacks in hard covers. Treats materials, tools; gives step-by-step instruction in how to collate a book, sew it, back it, make boards, etc. 261 illus. Appendices. 155pp. 5⅜ x 8.   20169-4   Paperbound $1.75

DESIGN MOTIFS OF ANCIENT MEXICO, J. Enciso. Nearly 90% of these 766 superb designs from Aztec, Olmec, Totonac, Maya, and Toltec origins are unobtainable elsewhere. Contains plumed serpents, wind gods, animals, demons, dancers, monsters, etc. Excellent applied design source. Originally $17.50. 766 illustrations, thousands of motifs. 192pp. 6⅛ x 9¼.
20084-1   Paperbound $2.25

A DIDEROT PICTORIAL ENCYCLOPEDIA OF TRADES AND INDUSTRY. Manufacturing and the Technical Arts in Plates Selected from "L'Encyclopédie ou Dictionnaire Raisonné des Sciences, des Arts, et des Métiers," of Denis Diderot, edited with text by C. Gillispie. Over 2000 illustrations on 485 full-page plates. Magnificent 18th-century engravings of men, women, and children working at such trades as milling flour, cheesemaking, charcoal burning, mining, silverplating, shoeing horses, making fine glass, printing, hundreds more, showing details of machinery, different steps in sequence, etc. A remarkable art work, but also the largest collection of working figures in print, copyright-free, for art directors, designers, etc. Two vols. 920pp. 9 x 12. Heavy library cloth.   22284-5, 22283-3   Two volume set $25.00

SILK SCREEN TECHNIQUES, J. Biegeleisen, M. Cohn. A practical step-by-step home course in one of the most versatile, least expensive graphic arts processes. How to build an inexpensive silk screen, prepare stencils, print, achieve special textures, use color, etc. Every step explained, diagrammed. 149 illustrations, 201pp. 6⅛ x 9¼.   20433-2   Paperbound $2.00

STICKS AND STONES, Lewis Mumford. An examination of forces influencing American architecture: the medieval tradition in early New England, the classical influence in Jefferson's time, the Brown Decades, the imperial facade, the machine age, etc. "A truly remarkable book," SAT. REV. OF LITERATURE. 2nd revised edition. 21 illus. xvii + 240pp. 5⅜ x 8.
20202-X   Paperbound $2.00

THE AUTOBIOGRAPHY OF AN IDEA, Louis Sullivan. The architect whom Frank Lloyd Wright called "the master," records the development of the theories that revolutionized America's skyline. 34 full-page plates of Sullivan's finest work. New introduction by R. M. Line. xiv + 335pp. 5⅜ x 8.
20281-X   Paperbound $2.50

GRAPHIC WORLDS OF PETER BRUEGEL THE ELDER,
H. A. Klein. 64 of the finest etchings and engravings made from
the drawings of the Flemish master Peter Bruegel. Every aspect
of the artist's diversified style and subject matter is represented,
with notes providing biographical and other background information. Excellent reproductions on opaque stock with nothing
on reverse side. 63 engravings, 1 woodcut. Bibliography. xviii +
289pp. 11⅜ x 8¼. 21132-0 Paperbound $3.50

THE COMPLETE WOODCUTS OF ALBRECHT DURER,
edited by Dr. Willi Kurth. Albrecht Dürer was a master in various media, but it was in woodcut design that his creative genius
reached its highest expression. Here are all of his extant woodcuts, a collection of over 300 great works, many of which are
not available elsewhere. An indispensable work for the art his-
torian and critic and all art lovers. 346 plates. Index. 285pp.
8½ x 12¼. 21097-9 Paperbound $3.00

GRAPHIC REPRODUCTION IN PRINTING, H. Curwen. A
behind-the-scenes account of the various processes of graphic
reproduction—relief, intaglio, stenciling, lithography, line
methods, continuous tone methods, photogravure, collotype—
and the advantages and limitations of each. Invaluable for all
artists, advertising art directors, commercial designers, adver-
tisers, publishers, and all art lovers who buy prints as a hobby.
137 illustrations, including 13 full-page plates, 10 in color. xvi +
171pp. 5¼ x 8½. 20512-6 Clothbound $7.50

WILD FOWL DECOYS, Joel Barber. Antique dealers, collectors,
craftsmen, hunters, readers of Americana, etc. will find this the
only thorough and reliable guide on the market today to this
unique folk art. It contains the history, cultural significance, regional design variations; unusual decoy lore; working plans for
constructing decoys; and loads of illustrations. 140 full-page
plates, 4 in color. 14 additional plates of drawings and plans by
the author. xxvii + 156pp. 7⅞ x 10¾. 20011-6 Paperbound $3.50

1800 WOODCUTS BY THOMAS BEWICK AND HIS SCHOOL.
This is the largest collection of first-rate pictorial woodcuts in
print—an indispensable part of the working library of every
commercial artist, art director, production designer, packaging
artist, craftsman, manufacturer, librarian, art collector, and
artist. And best of all, when you buy your copy of Bewick, you
buy the rights to reproduce individual illustrations—no permission needed, no acknowledgments, no clearance fees! Classified
index. Bibliography and sources. xiv + 246pp. 9 x 12.
20766-8 Paperbound $4.00

THE SCRIPT LETTER, Tommy Thompson. Prepared by a noted
authority, this is a thorough, straightforward course of instruction with advice on virtually every facet of the art of script
lettering. Also a brief history of lettering with examples from
early copy books and illustrations from present day advertising
and packaging. Copiously illustrated. Bibliography. 128pp.
6½ x 9⅛. 21311-0 Paperbound $1.25

VITRUVIUS: TEN BOOKS ON ARCHITECTURE. The most influential book in the history of architecture. 1st century A.D. Roman classic has influenced such men as Bramante, Palladio, Michelangelo, up to present. Classic principles of design, harmony, etc. Fascinating reading. Definitive English translation by Professor H. Morgan, Harvard. 344pp. 5⅜ x 8.

20645-9 Paperbound $2.50

HAWTHORNE ON PAINTING. Vivid re-creation, from students' notes, of instructions by Charles Hawthorne at Cape Cod School of Art. Essays, epigrammatic comments on color, form, seeing, techniques, etc. "Excellent," Time. 100pp. 5⅜ x 8.

20653-X Paperbound $1.25

THE HANDBOOK OF PLANT AND FLORAL ORNAMENT, *R. G. Hatton.* 1200 line illustrations, from medieval, Renaissance herbals, of flowering or fruiting plants: garden flowers, wild flowers, medicinal plants, poisons, industrial plants, etc. A unique compilation that probably could not be matched in any library in the world. Formerly "The Craftsman's Plant-Book." Also full text on uses, history as ornament, etc. 548pp. 6⅛ x 9¼.

20649-1 Paperbound $4.50

DECORATIVE ALPHABETS AND INITIALS, *Alexander Nesbitt.* 91 complete alphabets, over 3900 ornamental initials, from Middle Ages, Renaissance printing, baroque, rococo, and modern sources. Individual items copyright free, for use in commercial art, crafts, design, packaging, etc. 123 full-page plates. 3924 initials. 129pp. 7¾ x 10¾. 20544-4 Paperbound $2.75

METHODS AND MATERIALS OF THE GREAT SCHOOLS AND MASTERS, *Sir Charles Eastlake.* (Formerly titled "Materials for a History of Oil Painting.") Vast, authentic reconstruction of secret techniques of the masters, recreated from ancient manuscripts, contemporary accounts, analysis of paintings, etc. Oils, fresco, tempera, varnishes, encaustics. Both Flemish and Italian schools, also British and French. One of great works for art historians, critics; inexhaustible mine of suggestions, information for practicing artists. Total of 1025pp. 5⅜ x 8.

20718-8, 20719-6 Two volume set, Paperbound $7.00

BYZANTINE ART AND ARCHAEOLOGY, *O.M. Dalton.* Still most thorough work in English on Byzantine art forms throughout ancient and medieval world. Analyzes hundreds of pieces, covers sculpture, painting, mosaic, jewelry, textiles, architecture, etc. Historical development; specific examples; iconology and ideas; symbolism. A treasure-trove of material about one of most important art traditions, will supplement and expand any other book in area. Bibliography of over 2500 items. 457 illustrations. 747pp. 6⅛ x 9¼. 20776-5 Clothbound $8.50

THE HUMAN FIGURE, *J. H. Vanderpoel.* Not just a picture book, but a complete course by a famous figure artist. Extensive text, illustrated by 430 pencil and charcoal drawings of both male and female anatomy. 2nd enlarged edition. Foreword. 430 illus. 143pp. 6⅛ x 9¼. 20432-4 Paperbound $1.50

PENNSYLVANIA DUTCH AMERICAN FOLK ART, H. J. Kauffman. The originality and charm of this early folk art give it a special appeal even today, and surviving pieces are sought by collectors all over the country. Here is a rewarding introductory guide to the Dutch country and its household art, concentrating on pictorial matter—hex signs, tulip ware, weather vanes, interiors, paintings and folk sculpture, rocking horses and children's toys, utensils, Stiegel-type glassware, etc. "A serious, worthy and helpful volume," W. G. Dooley, N. Y. TIMES. Introduction. Bibliography. 279 halftone illustrations. 28 motifs and other line drawings. 1 map. 146pp. 7⅞ x 10¾.

21205-X Paperbound $2.00

DESIGN AND EXPRESSION IN THE VISUAL ARTS, J. F. A. Taylor. Here is a much needed discussion of art theory which relates the new and sometimes bewildering directions of 20th century art to the great traditions of the past. The first discussion of principle that addresses itself to the eye rather than to the intellect, using illustrations from Rembrandt, Leonardo, Mondrian, El Greco, etc. List of plates. Index. 59 reproductions. 5 color plates. 75 figures. x + 245pp. 5⅜ x 8½.

21195-9 Paperbound $2.25

THE ENJOYMENT AND USE OF COLOR, W. Sargent. Requiring no special technical know-how, this book tells you all about color and how it is created, perceived, and imitated in art. Covers many little-known facts about color values, intensities, effects of high and low illumination, complementary colors, and color harmonies. Simple do-it-yourself experiments and observations. 35 illustrations, including 6 full-page color plates. New color frontispiece. Index. x + 274 pp. 5⅜ x 8.

20944-X Paperbound $2.25

STYLES IN PAINTING, Paul Zucker. By comparing paintings of similar subject matter, the author shows the characteristics of various painting styles. You are shown at a glance the differences between reclining nudes by Giorgione, Velasquez, Goya, Modigliani; how a Byzantine portrait is unlike a portrait by Van Eyck, da Vinci, Dürer, or Marc Chagall; how the painting of landscapes has changed gradually from ancient Pompeii to Lyonel Feininger in our own century. 241 beautiful, sharp photographs illustrate the text. xiv + 338 pp. 5⅝ x 8¼.

20760-9 Paperbound $2.25

THE PRACTICE OF TEMPERA PAINTING, D. V. Thompson, Jr. Used in Egyptian and Minoan wall paintings and in much of the fine work of Giotto, Botticelli, Titian, and many others, tempera has long been regarded as one of the finest painting methods known. This is the definitive work on the subject by the world's outstanding authority. He covers the uses and limitations of tempera, designing, drawing with the brush, incising outlines, applying to metal, mixing and preserving tempera, varnishing and guilding, etc. Appendix, "Tempera Practice in Yale Art School" by Prof. L. E. York. 4 full page plates. 85 illustrations. x + 141pp. 5⅜ x 8½. 20343-3 Paperbound $1.75

VASARI ON TECHNIQUE, G. Vasari. Pupil of Michelangelo, outstanding biographer of Renaissance artists reveals technical methods of his day. Marble, bronze, fresco painting, mosaics, engraving, stained glass, rustic ware, etc. Only English translation, extensively annotated by G. Baldwin Brown. 18 plates. 342pp. 5⅜ x 8.   20717-X Paperbound $3.50

FOOT-HIGH LETTERS: A GUIDE TO LETTERING, M. Price. 28 15½ x 22½" plates, give classic Roman alphabet, one foot high per letter, plus 9 other 2" high letter forms for each letter. 16 page syllabus. Ideal for lettering classes, home study. 28 plates in box.   20238-9 $6.00

A HANDBOOK OF WEAVES, G. H. Oelsner. Most complete book of weaves, fully explained, differentiated, illustrated. Plain weaves, irregular, double-stitched, filling satins; derivative, basket, rib weaves; steep, broken, herringbone, twills, lace, tricot, many others. Translated, revised by S. S. Dale; supplement on analysis of weaves. Bible for all handweavers. 1875 illustrations. 410pp. 6⅛ x 9¼.   20209-7 Clothbound $7.50

JAPANESE HOMES AND THEIR SURROUNDINGS, E. S. Morse. Classic describes, analyses, illustrates all aspects of traditional Japanese home, from plan and structure to appointments, furniture, etc. Published in 1886, before Japanese architecture was contaminated by Western, this is strikingly modern in beautiful, functional approach to living. Indispensable to every architect, interior decorator, designer. 307 illustrations. Glossary. 410pp. 5⅝ x 8⅜.   20746-3 Paperbound $3.00

THE DRAWINGS OF HEINRICH KLEY. Uncut publication of long-sought-after sketchbooks of satiric, ironic iconoclast. Remarkable fantasy, weird symbolism, brilliant technique make Kley a shocking experience to layman, endless source of ideas, techniques for artist. 200 drawings, original size, captions translated. Introduction. 136pp. 6 x 9.   20024-8 Paperbound $2.00

COSTUMES OF THE ANCIENTS, Thomas Hope. Beautiful, clear, sharp line drawings of Greek and Roman figures in full costume, by noted artist and antiquary of early 19th century. Dress, armor, divinities, masks, etc. Invaluable sourcebook for costumers, designers, first-rate picture file for illustrators, commercial artists. Introductory text by Hope. 300 plates. 6 x 9.
20021-3 Paperbound $2.50

EPOCHS OF CHINESE AND JAPANESE ART, E. Fenollosa. Classic study of pre-20th century Oriental art, revealing, as does no other book, the important interrelationships between the art of China and Japan and their history and sociology. Illustrations include ancient bronzes, Buddhist paintings by Kobo Daishi, scroll paintings by Toba Sojo, prints by Nobusane, screens by Korin, woodcuts by Hokusai, Koryusai, Utamaro, Hiroshige and scores of other pieces by Chinese and Japanese masters. Biographical preface. Notes. Index. 242 illustrations. Total of lii + 439pp. plus 174 plates. 5⅝ x 8¼.
20364-6, 20265-4 Two-volume set, Paperbound $5.90

LANDSCAPE GARDENING IN JAPAN, Josiah Conder. A detailed picture of Japanese gardening techniques and ideas, the artistic principles incorporated in the Japanese garden, and the religious and ethical concepts at the heart of those principles. Preface. 92 illustrations, plus all 40 full-page plates from the Supplement. Index. xv + 299pp. 8⅜ x 11¼.

21216-5 Paperbound $3.50

DESIGN AND FIGURE CARVING, E. J. Tangerman. "Anyone who can peel a potato can carve," states the author, and in this unusual book he shows you how, covering every stage in detail from very simple exercises working up to museum-quality pieces. Terrific aid for hobbyists, arts and crafts counselors, teachers, those who wish to make reproductions for the commercial market. Appendix: How to Enlarge a Design. Brief bibliography. Index. 1298 figures. x + 289pp. 5⅜ x 8½.

21209-2 Paperbound $2.00

THE STANDARD BOOK OF QUILT MAKING AND COLLECTING, M. Ickis. Even if you are a beginner, you will soon find yourself quilting like an expert, by following these clearly drawn patterns, photographs, and step-by-step instructions. Learn how to plan the quilt, to select the pattern to harmonize with the design and color of the room, to choose materials. Over 40 full-size patterns. Index. 483 illustrations. One color plate. xi + 276pp. 6¾ x 9½. 20582-7 Paperbound $2.50

LOST EXAMPLES OF COLONIAL ARCHITECTURE, J. M. Howells. This book offers a unique guided tour through America's architectural past, all of which is either no longer in existence or so changed that its original beauty has been destroyed. More than 275 clear photos of old churches, dwelling houses, public buildings, business structures, etc. 245 plates, containing 281 photos and 9 drawings, floorplans, etc. New Index. xvii + 248pp. 7⅞ x 10¾. 21143-6 Paperbound $3.00

A HISTORY OF COSTUME, Carl Köhler. The most reliable and authentic account of the development of dress from ancient times through the 19th century. Based on actual pieces of clothing that have survived, using paintings, statues and other reproductions only where originals no longer exist. Hundreds of illustrations, including detailed patterns for many articles. Highly useful for theatre and movie directors, fashion designers, illustrators, teachers. Edited and augmented by Emma von Sichart. Translated by Alexander K. Dallas. 594 illustrations. 464pp. 5⅛ x 7⅛.

21030-8 Paperbound $3.00

Dover publishes books on commercial art, art history, crafts, design, art classics; also books on music, literature, science, mathematics, puzzles and entertainments, chess, engineering, biology, philosophy, psychology, languages, history, and other fields. For free circulars write to Dept. DA, Dover Publications, Inc., 180 Varick St., New York, N.Y. 10014.